Lessons
from
Mother Goose

Lessons
from
Mother Goose

Elaine Commins, M.Ed.

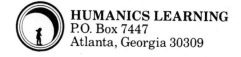

HUMANICS LEARNING
P.O. Box 7447
Atlanta, Georgia 30309

HUMANICS LEARNING
P.O. Box 7447
Atlanta, Georgia 30309

First Printing 1989

PRINTED IN THE UNITED STATES OF AMERICA

Library of Congress Cataloging-in-Publication Data

LIBRARY OF CONGRESS
Library of Congress Cataloging-in-Publication Data

Commins, Elaine.
  Lessons from Mother Goose / by Elaine Commins.
    p.   cm.
  Bibliography: p.
  ISBN 0-89334-110-X
  1. Children's literature—History and criticism. 2. Creative activities and seat work. I. Title.
PN1009.A1C64 1989
398′.8—dc19   87-30130
                                                        CIP

TABLE OF CONTENTS

INTRODUCTION

Nursery rhymes are part of our heritage. They enrich the literature of the young child with colorful tales, historical lore, and fantasy. In addition, they provide a number of valuable learning experiences such as: introducing the child to the world of poetry through rhythm and rhyming; teaching subjects such as counting and the alphabet; and even touching on simple lessons in morality. But above all, they are peppered with whimsey and humor which please and delight the listener.

For centuries, scholars have been fascinated with the historical background of nursery rhymes. Some find no meanings to the jingles, believing them to be of such ancient lineage as to remain an unsolvable mystery. Others state that fewer of the nursery rhymes come from antiquity than is popularly supposed and they are steeped in known historical facts. We do know that, with the exception of "Old King Cole," the periods in which most of the verses attained popularity were the following:

PLANTAGENET

Edward, the Black Prince
Henry V (House of Lancaster)
Richard III (House of York)

TUDOR

Henry VII
Henry VIII
Edward VI
Mary I
Elizabeth I

STUART

James I
Charles I

THE PROTECTORATE

Charles II
James II
William III
Anne

HANOVER

George I

Whatever their origins, the rhymes in this book are for enjoyment as well as a means of promoting intellectual and creative development. Each rhyme has activities to accompany it, which are designed to enlarge and expand on the literary fun through coordinated lessons and games. Areas of learning include art, language arts, dramatics, mathematics, science social studies, music, and physical education.

Old Mother Goose

ld Mother Goose when she wanted to wander
Rode through the air on a very fine gander.

Mother Goose had a house built in the woods,
An owl at the door for a sentinel stood.

France, the United States, and England all have legends which give them claim to the person of Mother Goose.

Contes de ma Mere L'Oye (Tales from Mother Goose), a book of fairy tales, was published by Charles Perrault in 1697. This was the first time the name of Mother Goose appeared in print. The French also attribute the name of Mother Goose to "goose-footed Bertha," wife of Robert II of France. She is portrayed as spinning cloth while children "clustered about listening to her tales."[1]

In the Old Granary Burying Ground in Boston, there are several tombstones dating back from about 1700 with the name "Goose" on them. One in particular, is pointed out to be that of Mother Goose.[2]

Around 1710 in London, the name "Mother Goose" was first used in Robert Powell's puppet shows. Between 1760 and 1765, the Newberry edition of *Mother Goose's Melody* appeared. This was the first printed collection of Mother Goose nursery rhymes.[3]

---

1. Katherine Elwes Thomas, *The Real Personages of Mother Goose,* Lothrop, 1930, p. 28.
2. May Hill Arbuthnot, *Children and Books,* Scott, Foresman and Co., 3rd Edition, p. 78.
3. Ibid., p. 77.

NURSERY RHYME BOOKLETS

Each child is given a large (12″ × 18″) folded sheet of construction paper. On one side the child draws and colors a Mother Goose figure. This will be the cover of a nursery rhyme booklet.

Then, given 8½″ × 11″ paper for the inside pages, children draw a different nursery rhyme on each page. Children should print the titles of each rhyme or the rhyme itself on each page, if possible.

ANIMAL GUESSING GAME
Language Arts

Children are asked if they can think of another nursery rhyme which mentions a goose.

> *Answer: Goosey, goosey gander, whither shall I wander?*
> *Upstairs and downstairs in my lady's chamber.*
> *There I met an old man who would not say his prayers.*
> *I took him by the left leg and threw him down the stairs.*

Children are asked to name other animals that are found in nursery rhymes. The following are possible answers:

cat *(Hey, diddle diddle, the cat and the fiddle)*
cow *(. . . the cow jumped over the moon)*
dog *(. . . the little dog laughed . . .)*
pig *(To market, to market to buy a fat pig)*
spider *(Little Miss Muffet)*
mice *(Three blind mice)*
mouse *(Hickory, dickory dock)*
sheep *(Little Bo-Peep has lost her sheep)*
blackbirds *(Sing a song of sixpence)*
lamb *(Mary had a little lamb)*
ladybird *(Ladybird, ladybird fly away home)*
horse *(Ride a cockhorse to Bamberry Cross)*
kittens *(The three little kittens)*

KEEP THE BEAT
Rhythm

Using a drum or a tom-tom, the teacher beats out the rhythm to "Old Mother Goose" while saying the rhyme. Children clap their hands with the beat. Children may then take turns beating the tom-tom to the rhythm of other nursery rhymes.

PANTOMIME
Dramatics

Children take turns, singly or in groups, silently acting out the different nursery rhymes. The rest of the children try to guess which rhyme they are watching.

Old King Cole

O ld King Cole was a merry old soul,
And a merry old soul was he;
He called for his pipe,
And he called for his bowl,
And he called for his fiddlers three.

And every fiddler had a fine fiddle,
And a very fine fiddle had he.
Twee tweedle dee, tweedle dee, went the
    fiddlers.
Oh, there's none so rare
As can compare
With King Cole and his fiddlers three.

As legends state, Cole was a popular king around 200 A.D. in Britain. His daughter was a skilled musician and he enjoyed listening to music.[1]

The Old King Cole jingle is actually regarded as the beginning of nursery rhymes in England.[2]

---

1. World Book Encyclopedia, Vol 13, 1972, p. 699.
2. Katherine Elwes Thomas, *The Real Personages of Mother Goose*, Lothrop, 1930, p. 35.

Humanics

CROWNS
Art

Materials: large construction paper (12″ × 18″)   glitter, paint and paste
hole puncher   a cardboard pattern of a crown
string or yarn

Method: Children trace the crown pattern on a piece of construction paper, cut it out and decorate it with paint and glitter. A hole is punched on each end of the crown and string inserted through each hole.

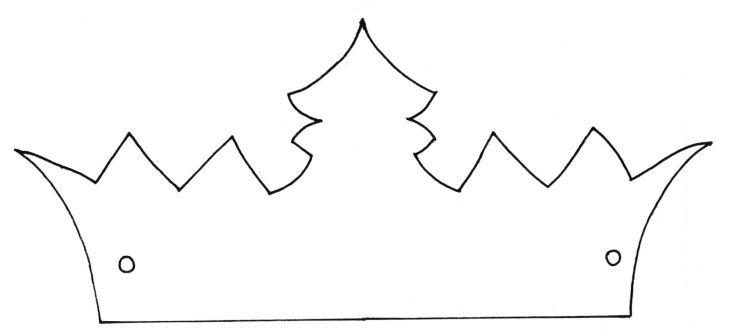

CLAY BOWLS
Art

Materials: Each child is given approximately 1 pound of clay.

Method: Each child fashions a bowl similar to one they think a king might have used. If a kiln is available, bowls may be baked and then taken home as gifts for a parent.

ACTING
Dramatics

Children act out the rhyme using accessories they have made (such as a crown, bowl, or musical instrument).

RHYMING WORDS
Language Arts

Either orally in a group or on their papers, children are asked to think of words that rhyme with each of the words of the first line of the jingle. For example:

> *old*—fold, mold, sold, bold
> *king*—ring, sing, bring, thing
> *Cole*—soul, poll, toll, roll, hole
> *was*—does, fuzz, because

CREATIVE THINKING
Language Arts

The teacher suggests some thought-provoking ideas about the nursery rhyme which she gives to the children. For example:

> *What do they think was in the bowl?*
> *What would happen if the fiddlers didn't come?*
> *How old was King Cole?*
> *Where did they all live?*

RUBBER BAND INSTRUMENTS
Music

Materials:
Various-sized cardboard boxes
Assorted rubber bands

Method:
Boxes and rubber bands are placed on a table. Children experiment with them by placing one or more rubber bands on the boxes to form a musical instrument. They may play their stringed instruments in a group. Instruments may be arranged according to pitch, (high or low).

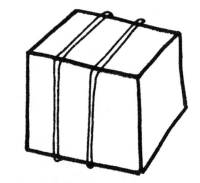

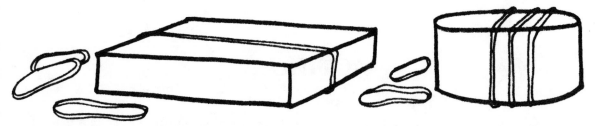

Rain, Rain Go Away

Rain, rain, go away,
Come again some other day.

Rain, rain, go away,
Little children want to play.

Rain, rain, go to Spain
Never show your face again.

This rhyme may be the oldest one known. It is claimed by some that a version of it was chanted by children in ancient Greece.[1]

Many variations exist, but the first verse is generally considered the one that has been used universally.

---

1. Mutherin, Jennifer, editor, *Popular Nursery Rhymes,* Granada Publishing, 1984, p. 105.

Humanics

UMBRELLAS
Art

Materials: a pattern for umbrellas
a variety of wallpaper sheets
pencils
scissors

Method: A table is prepared upon which children are offered umbrella patterns and a variety of wallpaper patterns. They are asked to cut out pairs of matching umbrellas.

The pairs of umbrellas are kept in a box. Children take turns matching the pairs.

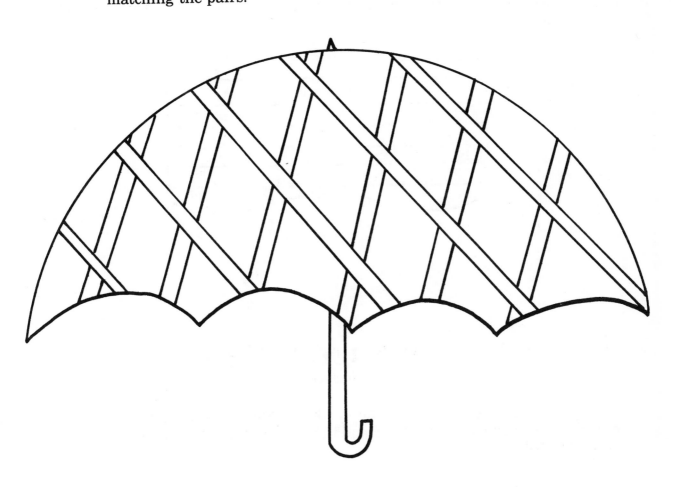

RAIN POEMS
Language Arts

Read rain poems to the children and have them draw pictures of what they have heard.

RAINY DAY ACTIVITIES
Language Arts

Discuss rainy day activities with the class. A list with simple drawings may be written on a chart tablet showing each child's preference.

MEASURE RAINFALL
Mathematics

A chart is prepared which has a column for the date and the amount of rainfall that is measured. A measuring cup is placed outdoors on rainy days and the water level is measured and recorded.

Rainfall	
date	amount
Jan . 26	½"
Feb . 6	1"
Feb . 7	¼"

WEATHER NEWS
Science

Children are asked to bring in the weather section of the daily paper for one week. Each day's rainfall is observed and the cities that get rainfall are listed on the chalkboard.

London Bridge

London Bridge has fallen down,
Fallen down, fallen down,
London Bridge has fallen down,
My fair lady.

Build it up with wood and clay,
Wood and clay, wood and clay,
Build it up with wood and clay,
My fair lady.

Wood and clay will wash away,
Wash away, wash away,
Wood and clay will wash away,
My fair lady.

Build it up with bricks and mortar,
Bricks and mortar, bricks and mortar,

Build it up with bricks and mortar,
My fair lady.

Bricks and mortar will not stay,
Will not stay, will not stay,
Bricks and mortar will not stay,
My fair lady.

Build it up with iron and steel,
Iron and steel, iron and steel,
Build it up with iron and steel,
My fair lady.

Iron and steel will bend and bow,
Bend and bow, bend and bow,
Iron and steel will bend and bow,
My fair lady.

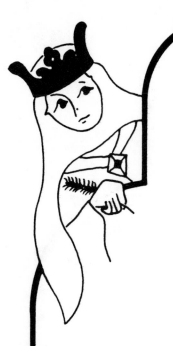

Build it up with silver and gold,
Silver and gold, silver and gold,
Build it up with silver and gold,
My fair lady.

Silver and gold will be stolen away,
Stolen away, stolen away,
Silver and gold will be stolen away,
My fair lady.

Set a man to watch all night,
Watch all night, watch all night,
Set a man to watch all night,
My fair lady.

Suppose the man should fall asleep,
Fall asleep, fall asleep,
Suppose the man should fall asleep?
My fair lady.

Give him a pipe to smoke all night,
Smoke all night, smoke all night,
Give him a pipe to smoke all night,
My fair lady.

Many London bridges have fallen down over the years.
According to legend, the first bridges were made of wood. The last
wooden bridge was destroyed by King Olaf and his Norsemen in the
eleventh century.

A stone bridge was begun in 1176 by the priest Peter of
Colechurch. As you can see by the illustration, houses were
constructed along the bridge in those early times.[1]

---

1. Salzman, L. F. *English Life in the Middle Ages,* Oxford University
Press, 1972, p. 270.

Lessons from Mother Goose

BRIDGE PICTURES
Art

Materials: toothpicks
glue
colored construction paper
pencils, crayons or felt-tipped markers

Method: Children first draw pictures of bridges on their papers. Toothpicks are then glued over the drawings. After the glue has dried, they may further decorate their pictures with drawings.

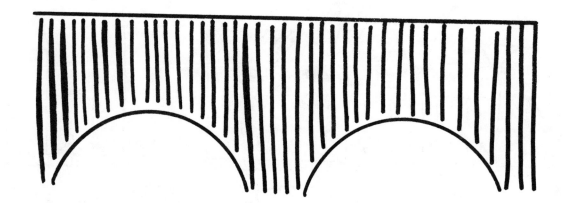

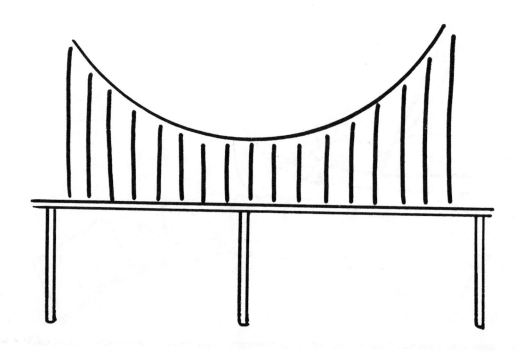

DISCUSSING BRIDGES
Language Arts

Why do we need bridges? Describe the different kind of bridges you have seen or heard of, i.e., bridges over water, bridges over expressways, bridges over a ravine, pontoon bridges, swinging rope bridges, covered bridges, etc.

THREE BILLY GOATS GRUFF
Language Arts

Tell the story of the "Three Billy Goats Gruff." They had to cross a bridge to get to the other side of the mountain. Who lived under the bridge?

BRIDGE POSTER
Social Studies

A large piece of poster board is titled "Bridges," and the children are given old magazines to look for "bridge pictures." These are cut out and pasted on the poster-board. Children may also bring pictures of bridges from home. When complete, the poster may be tacked on a bulletin board or taped on the wall.

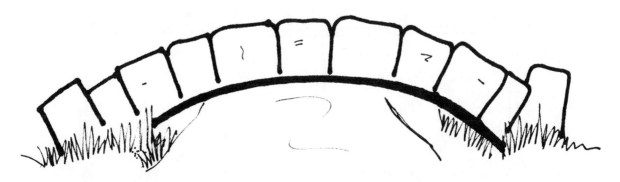

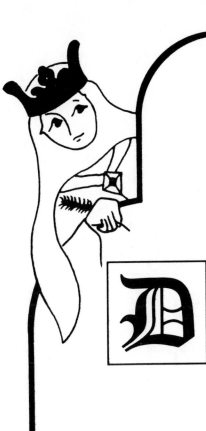

Doctor Foster

octor Foster went to Gloucester
In a shower of rain;
He stepped in a puddle,
Right up to his middle,
And never went there again.

Many believe that Dr. Foster was Edward I. On a visit to Gloucester, the king sank so deep in a puddle that planks had to be put down so his horse could regain its footing. He was so angry that he vowed never to visit Gloucester again.[1]

---

1. Mutherin, Jennifer, editor, *Popular Nursery Rhymes*, Granada Publishing, 1984, p. 29.

Humanics

RAINBOW PICTURES
Art and Science

Materials: one or two shallow glass dishes ½ filled with water
sunlight
crayons
paper

Method: A shallow glass containing water is placed in direct sunlight. Bands of colored light will be reflected on walls, ceiling, floor, desks, etc. Children will first identify the colors they see and then draw their own rainbow pictures.

WATER PLAY
Mathematics

Materials: two large dishpans
water
measuring spoons and cups
a funnel
a dipper
a sieve
wire whisk
egg beater
empty squeeze bottles
large Turkish towel

Method: A large Turkish towel is placed on a table to absorb excess water. Dishpans are set on the towel. One dishpan is filled about ¾ full of water. Children are encouraged to experiment using the tools provided. They may keep records such as the number of pints it takes to fill a quart jar, etc.

MAKING RAIN
Science

The teacher fills a whistling tea kettle about ¼ full of water. It is placed on a stove or a hot plate. When it whistles, a dinner-sized plate containing ice cubes is held over the steam. (Do not use a small plate as there is a danger of getting scalded.) Droplets of water will form and fall.

Children will discuss what they observed. The conclusion that warm air rising and colliding with cold air causes rain can be reached.

WEATHER REPORTER
Science

Children are asked to watch the weather reporter on television. The following morning, the teacher tapes a large U.S. map and/or a state map on the chalkboard.

One child is selected to give the weather report that day. This same activity may be repeated another day to give other children the opportunity to be the weather reporter.

Humpty Dumpty

Humpty Dumpty sat on a wall,
Humpty Dumpty had a great fall.
All the King's horses
And all the King's men
Couldn't put Humpty together again!

When Edward V became king he was only 12 years old and considered too young to rule. Therefore, his uncle Richard was named Protector of the Realm to rule temporarily until Richard was of age.

But Richard was very ambitious and wanted to be king also. He placed the young king and his little brother in the Tower of London where they both mysteriously disappeared. Then Richard III, "humpback Dick," became the new king in 1483.

There were those who bitterly opposed Richard III, and two years later Henry Tudor, leader of the opposition, raised an army to fight the king. A great battle was fought on Bosworth Field. Richard was killed and his army defeated.

Although Richard's forces had been superior, neither his many men nor their fine horses could put him back on the throne again. Katherine Elwes Thomas believes that Richard III was Humpty-Dumpty.[1]

---

1. Katherine Elwes Thomas, *The Real Personages of Mother Goose,* Lothrop, 1930, p. 39.

Humanics

EGG PUZZLES
Art

Materials: vari-colored construction paper
felt marker
scissors
large oval pattern   See Page 26 for Pattern

Method: Each child selects one of the colored pieces of construction paper, traces the oval pattern on it, and then marks it off into segments with a felt marking pen. The oval (egg) is cut out and then the segments are cut out to form a puzzle. Children take turns working their own and each other's puzzles. Using various colors helps children identify their own puzzle.

CREATING THINKING
Language Arts

Discuss why Humpty Dumpty couldn't be put back together again. What if he could be put back together? The teacher brings an egg to school, cracks it, and demonstrates the discussion.

EGG MATCHING GAME
Mathematics

The teacher cuts out 10 posterboard eggs. Each is divided in half by a jagged line. The matching halves are marked; one half with numbers, the other half with corresponding dots. They are then cut out along the jagged line. Children fit the corresponding pieces together.

See page 27 for Pattern

COMPARATIVE COOKING
Science

For one week, the teacher brings 3 or 4 eggs each day and cooks them in a different way. For example: Monday, scrambled eggs; Tuesday, hard boiled eggs; Wednesday, soft boiled eggs; Thursday, fried eggs; Friday, egg salad.

Children are given a small taste each day. A chart is prepared, and children select the method of cooking that they preferred.

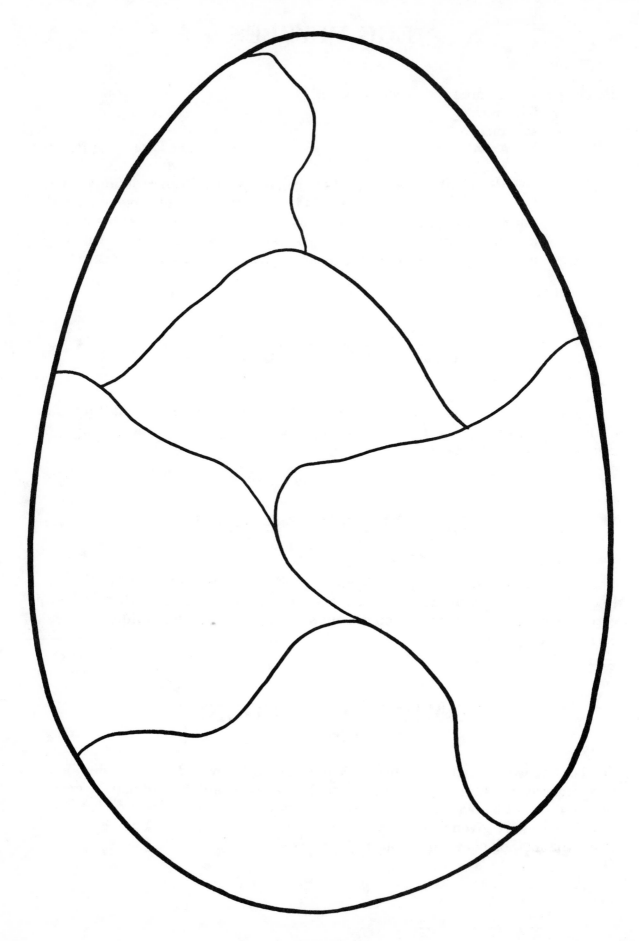

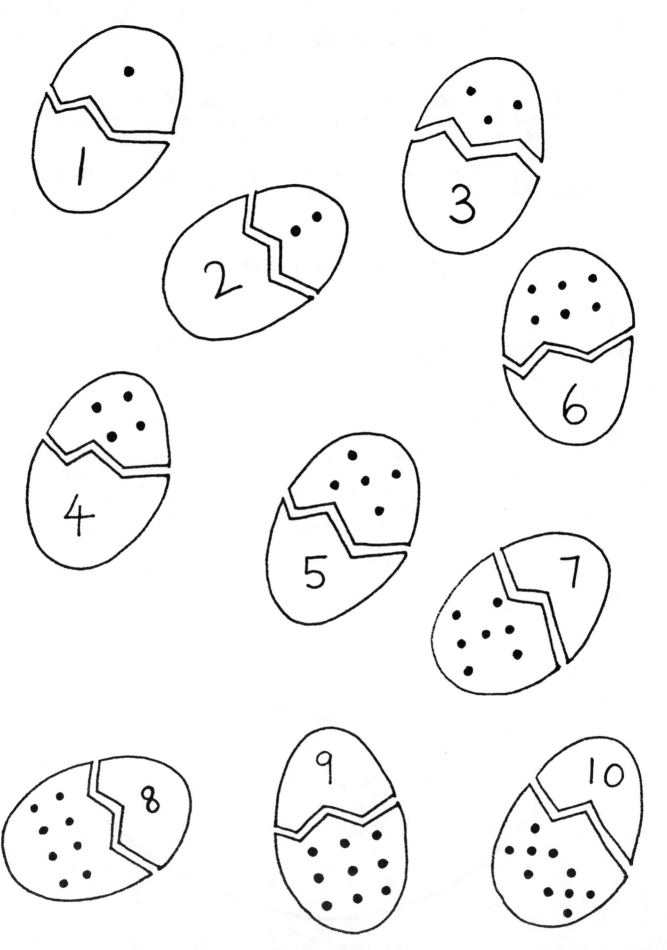

EGG CONTAINER
Science

Each child is asked to design a small container in which an egg can be held safely when dropped from the top of a sliding board. Materials that can be used are shredded newspaper, styrofoam, cotton, etc. Children are encouraged to use their own ideas.

All containers may be tested by the class. Winners are those whose eggs did not break. Some kind of reward is suggested.

HUMPTY DUMPTY PLANTER
Science

Materials: a brick
a paper baking cup
¾ of an egg shell
dirt
grass seed
felt tip markers

Method: The paper baking cup is glued to the brick and the egg shell is glued inside it. With felt tip markers, the teacher draws a face on the egg shell. Dirt is placed inside the egg shell and grass seed planted in it. The brick is placed in a sunny spot in the classroom and lightly watered each day with a spoon by a student. As the grass grows it looks like Humpty Dumpty's hair.

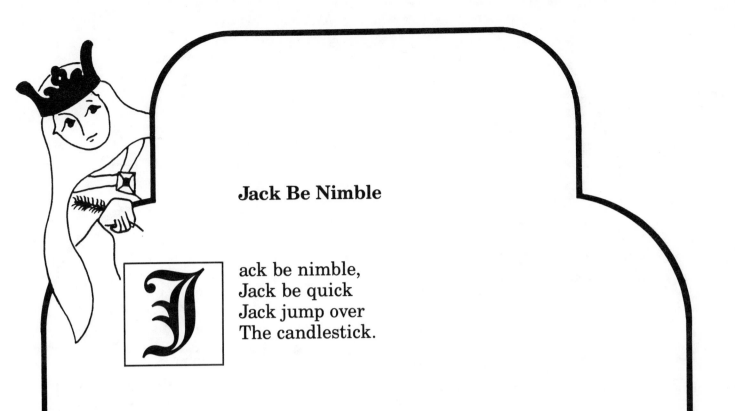

Jack Be Nimble

Jack be nimble,
Jack be quick
Jack jump over
The candlestick.

Candle-leaping was both a sport and a type of fortune telling that was practiced in England for some centuries. A lighted candlestick was placed on the floor and, if the light was not extinguished while a person jumped over it, good luck was supposed to follow the person through the coming year.[1]

---

1. Iona and Peter Opie, *The Oxford Dictionary of Nursery Rhymes,* Clarendon Press, 1973, pp. 226, 227.

WAX RELIEF PAINTING
Art

Materials: manila paper
a wax candle
tempera paint

Method: Children are given a candle to draw a design on their paper. After the design is finished, they paint over the entire surface of the paper with very watery tempera. A picture will emerge.

CREATIVE DISCUSSION
Language Arts

What would happen if Jack didn't jump high enough and tipped over the candle? Talk about good fires and bad fires.

Have the children draw two pictures of the same subject, one before and one after a fire. Let each child explain his/her picture in front of the group.

FIRE NEEDS AIR
Science

The teacher lights two candles. A glass jar is placed over one of them. The children observe what happens to the flame. Discuss why it went out.

HEAT RISES
Science

The teacher lights one candle. Under close supervision, children take turns holding a hand near the side of the candle, under the candle and over the candle. Which position felt hotter?

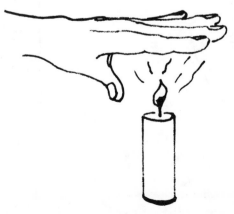

CANDLE MAKING
Science

Materials: double boiler
paraffin
crayons
cotton string
clothesline
clothespins

Method: Heat and melt paraffin in a double boiler. An empty coffee can may be used as the upper pot. Water should be just warm enough to melt paraffin. Do not allow paraffin to boil as it will burn. Do not heat over direct flame as it might ignite. Color may be added by dropping some broken wax crayons into the paraffin.

Cut cotton string two inches longer than the depth of the pot or coffee can. The child dips the string into the hot paraffin. The paraffin will adhere to the string.

Remove and hang up by the string, or wick, to dry. A clothesline and clothespins are acceptable. Repeat the process several times depending on the thickness of candle that is desired.

Note: to finish the process in one operation, first dip the wick into the melted paraffin, then in a second coffee can filled with ice-water, then back in the wax, etc.

Little Jack Horner

L ittle Jack Horner
Sat in a corner
Eating a Christmas pie.
He stuck in his thumb
And pulled out a plum
And said, "What a good boy am I!"

When the Bishop of Gastonberry sent his steward Jack Horner to King Henry VIII with title deeds for 12 estates, they were safely hidden in a Christmas pie. Jack lifted the pie crust and craftily kept one of the deeds to an estate for himself. To this day the Horner family owns it at Mills Park, England.[1]

---

1. *World Book Encyclopedia,* Vol. 13, 1966, pg. 698.

PLAY-DOUGH PLUMS
Art

Materials: pink play-dough
blue play-dough

Method: Children are given equal portions of pink and blue play dough. They knead the two colors together to create purple. They then roll it into plums.

NONSENSE RHYMES
Language Arts

The teacher suggests other body parts and children finish the rhymes. For example:

He stuck in his *nose* and pulled out a *rose*.
He stuck in his *eye* and pulled out a *tie*.
He stuck in his *ear* and pulled out a *deer*.
He stuck in his *hair* and pulled out a *bear*.
He stuck in his *chin* and pulled out a *pin*.
He stuck in his *arm* and pulled out a *charm*.
He stuck in his *chest* and pulled out a *vest*.
He stuck in his *tummy* and pulled out a *mummy*.
He stuck in his *knee* and pulled out a *tree*.
He stuck in his *feet* and pulled out a *treat*.
He stuck in his *toe* and pulled out a *bow*.

PRUNES
Science

A prune is a sweet plum that has been dried. To illustrate the discussion, the teacher might bring a box of pitted prunes to school and pass one to each child.

Prunes are very healthful because they contain vitamins and iron. Most of the prunes in the United States come from California.

After each child has tasted a raw prune, the remainder could be stewed. (Follow directions on the box.) Children could then compare the taste of stewed prunes to raw prunes. If fresh plums are available, they could also be sampled for comparison.

LITTLE JACK HORNER
Music

Lit-tle Jack Horn - er sat in a cor - ner, Eat-ing a Christ-mas pie;____ He put in his thumb, and pulled out a plum, And said "what a good boy am I."____

Sing A Song Of Sixpence

ing a song of sixpence,
A pocket full of rye.
Four and twenty blackbirds baked in a pie.
When the pie was open the birds began to
 sing.
Wasn't that a dainty dish to set before the
 king?

The king was in his counting house
Counting out his money.
The queen was in the parlor eating bread
 and honey.
The maid was in the garden hanging out the
 clothes.
Along came a blackbird and pecked off her
 nose!

"Sing a song of sixpence" is a little jingle about Henry VIII. He is happily humming over his confiscated revenues from the abbeys. The "pocket full of rye" represents rich grain fields, while "four and twenty blackbirds" are the deeds baked into Jack Horner's pie.

The queen who was blithely eating bread and honey soon gave way to her successor—Ann Boleyn, the lovely French maid who enticed Henry. But Ann's fate, alas, was sealed by the blackbird who snipped off more than just a nose.[1]

---

1. Katherine Elwes Thomas, *The Real Personages of Mother Goose*, Lothrop, 1930, pp. 68, 69.

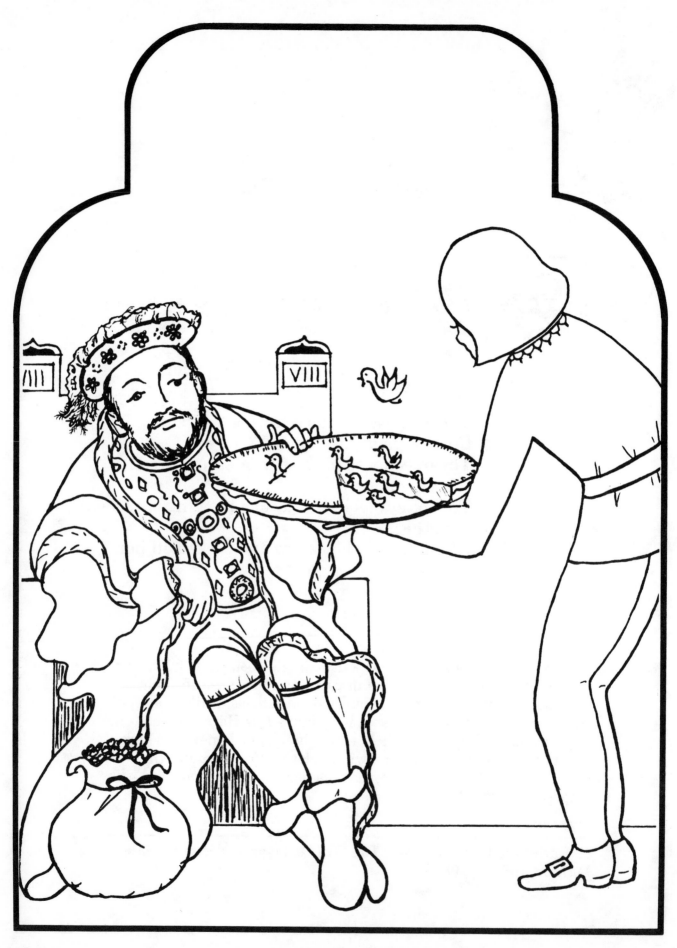

Humanics

HOW MANY BLACKBIRDS
Art

Materials: cardboard patterns of a bird
               black construction paper
               chalk for tracing
               scissors

Method: A bulletin board with a light-colored background is prepared by the teacher. It contains a caption and a "sign-up" sheet.

       Children trace and cut out as many blackbirds as they desire, then post them on the bulletin board. After all the birds are posted, each child counts the birds and records his/her findings on the "sign-up" sheet.

       After a few days, when all have signed, the birds are removed, counted by the class and teacher together, and the student(s) with the correct answer or nearest answer is the winner.[1]

---

1. Elaine Commins, *Bloomin Bulletin Boards,* Humanics Ltd., 1984, p. 57.

WORDS BEGINNING WITH "S"
Language Arts

This is a circle time activity. The teacher begins by saying, "Sing a song of sixpence, a pocket full of _____." (A word beginning with "s" is inserted here, i.e, *sun*.) Each child then has a turn, and repeats the first words of the rhyme but fills in his/her own word beginning with "s."

MATCHING BLACKBIRDS
Mathematics

The teacher cuts out ten 5″ × 7″ pieces of oak tag or poster board.

Each piece is divided unevenly into three sections. One section contains numerals from one to ten. Another section contains the written word for the same numeral and the last section contains a corresponding number of black birds. The sections are cut out and children take turns fitting the sections together. For ease in handling, the cards may be stored in a cigar box.

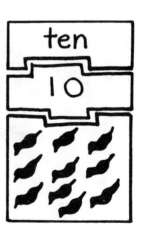

APPLE CRISP
PIE WITH BLACKBIRDS
Science

Ingredients: 10–14 large cooking apples, peeled, cored, and thinly sliced
½ cup granulated sugar
½ cup brown sugar
½ tsp cinnamon (more if desired)
several dashes of nutmeg
juice of 1 lemon
24 raisins

Children help peel the apples. Arrange apple slices in large greased Pyrex pan. They will be piled very high. The sugars, cinnamon, nutmeg, and lemon juice are sprinkled on each of the layers. Last, the "four and twenty" raisins are dribbled on and mixed in with the apple slices.

Topping: 1 stick of soft margarine   ½ cup of sugar
¾ to 1 cup of flour   ½ cup of mashed pecans.
dash of salt

Children can mash pecans. They should be placed in a clean kitchen towel and a rolling pin rolled over them. Mix ingredients together and sprinkle over apple mixture. Bake at 375 degrees for about 1 hour. Eat while warm. Children try to find a blackbird (raisin) in their portion. This "pie" can serve an entire class of 15 to 18 children.

LOOKING FOR OCCUPATIONS
Social Studies

The children and teacher dissect each line of the rhyme, looking for a suggested job. For example:

Sing a song of sixpence. Who sings songs? A singer.
A pocket full of rye. Who grows rye? A farmer.
Four and twenty blackbirds baked in a pie. Who bakes pies? A baker.
When the pie was open the birds began to sing. Who serves pies? A waiter.
Wasn't that a dainty dish to set before the king? What does a king do? He rules.
The king was in his counting house What is a counting house? An accountant's office.
Counting out his money. Who counts money? A banker.
The queen was in the parlor eating bread and honey. What does a queen do? She helps the king rule.
The maid was in the garden hanging out the clothes. What do maids do? They clean, cook, and wash.
Along came a blackbird and pecked off her nose. Who would be called to fix her nose? A doctor.

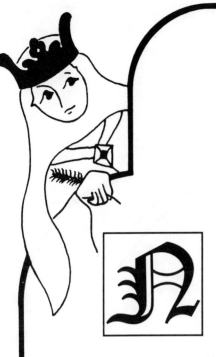

Needles And Pins

eedles and pins,
Needles and pins,
When a man marries,
His trouble begins

"Needles and Pins" is a sing-song ditty that was popular during the time of King Henry VIII. It reflected on the many unhappy marriages of the king.

Pins were introduced into England by Katherine Howard, the king's fifth wife. Although they were extremely expensive, pins were in great demand, and so the expression "pin money" arose.[1]

---

1. Katherine Elwes Thomas, *The Real Personages of Mother Goose*, Lothrop, 1930, pp. 75, 76.

44

SEWING
Art

Materials: paper plates
plastic embroidery needles or extra large metal needles
yarn
hole puncher

Method: The child or the teacher punches holes around the edge of a paper plate. Using a needle that has been theaded with yarn, the child stitches around or across the plate as he or she pleases. The end of the thread may be stapled to the plate to hold it down.

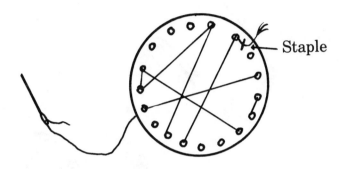

Staple

PIN CUSHIONS
Art

Materials: 5″ felt squares (2 per child)
hole puncher
plastic embroidery needles or extra large metal needles
yarn
cotton for stuffing

Method: Holding two felt squares together evenly, the teacher or the child punches holes (approximately 1″ apart) all around the edges.
    The teacher threads the needle with yarn and ties a knot at the first hole. The child then sews the two pieces of felt together by using a "whip" stitch through each hole. After three sides of the squares have been stitched together, the cotton stuffing is inserted and then the fourth side is stitched.

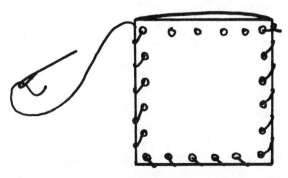

Lessons from Mother Goose

FASTENERS
Language Arts

The teacher asks the children to think of things that are "fasteners." For example, they try to think of objects that hold things together. The teacher might first suggest a safety pin and how it can be used. As children volunteer answers, the teacher makes a simple drawing of each object plus its name on the chart tablet.

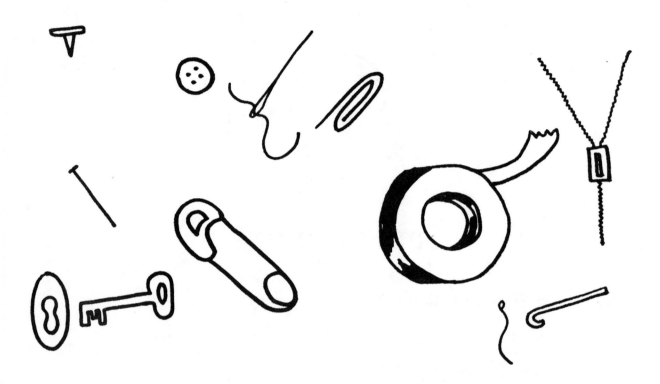

FINDING "N'S" and "P'S"
Language Arts

Each child is given a column (preferably large print) from a magazine, and a light-colored marking pen or highlighting pen. The "n's" and "p's" are colored in, and all the papers are then tacked on a bulletin board.

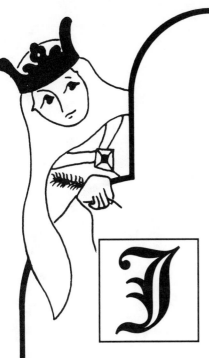

Jack And Jill

J ack and Jill
Went up the hill
To fetch a pail of water.
Jack fell down
And broke his crown
And Jill came tumbling after.

The woodcut illustrating Jack and Jill in *Mother Goose's Melody,* 1765, showed two boys rather than a boy and a girl.[1]

Around 1835, John Bellenden Ker, a scholar who delved into the histories of nursery rhymes, said that Jack and Jill were actually two priests. The pail of water was the "burial perquisite—one of the principle bonuses of the priests at that time. The water used here is in the meaning of a fee."[2]

Katherine Elwes Thomas enlarged upon Ker's position by stating that Jack and Jill were Cardinal Wolsey and Bishop Tarbes who went to France to arrange for the marriage of Mary Tudor, King Henry VIII's oldest daughter, to the French King.[3] The marriage plans fell flat, however, just as Jack and Jill fell flat when they came tumbling down the hill.

---

1. William S. Baring-Gould, and Ceil Baring-Gould, *The Annotated Mother Goose,* Bramhall House, 1962, p. 60.
2. Ibid., p. 62.
3. Ibid., p. 62.

Humanics

BEFORE AND AFTER PICTURES
Art

Material: manila paper
pencils
crayons and/or felt tip markers

Method: Children are asked to draw and color two pictures of Jack and Jill—one going up the hill and the other going down. The pictures should be labelled and posted on the bulletin board.

ACTING OUT JACK AND JILL
Dramatics

Children take turns acting out the rhyme. Using large building blocks, children build steps to represent a hill. They make their own costumes using clothing from the "dress-up box" or large paper bags. Old clothing may be donated from older children or purchased at Good Will.

CREATIVE THINKING
Language Arts

The teacher asks the following questions after reading the rhyme:
"What is Jack's crown?"
"What is a pail?"
"What happened to the water when Jack fell down?"
"After Jack broke his crown, what do you think he did?"
After all have answered, read the next verse of the rhyme:

> Then up Jack got
> And home did trot
> As fast as he could caper.
> He jumped into bed
> And bandaged his head
> With vinegar and brown paper.

"Where did Jill go after Jack broke his crown?"
"Did she get hurt, too?"
"Was her mother angry? Why?"

TUMBLING
Physical Education

Discuss tumbling with the children. If possible, introduce tumbling in the classroom. A mat is required for the following exercises:

Forward Roll (Somersault): Begin in a squatting position with knees apart, hands on mat between knees. Roll forward and over.

Backward Roll: Squat, keep back curved, roll back placing hands on floor behind head. Push with hands and continue to roll until completely flipped over.

Side Roll: Child rolls sideways from one end of the mat to the other.

Other movements for the mat: Slither on your tummy from one end to the other, scoot backwards on your bottom from one end to the other, walk on your knees from one end to the other, etc.

JACK AND JILL
Music

Jack and Jill went up the hill, To fetch a pail of wa - ter;

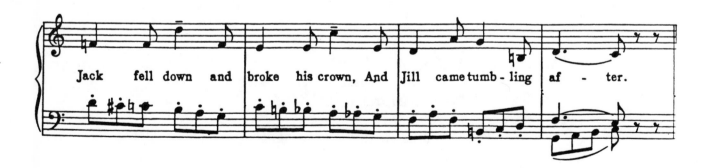

Jack fell down and broke his crown, And Jill came tumb - ling af - ter.

Humanics

Little Boy Blue

L ittle Boy Blue
Come blow your horn
The sheep's in the meadow;
The cow's in the corn.
Where is the boy who looks after the sheep?
He's under the haystack, fast asleep.
Will you wake him?
No, not I, for if I do
He'll be sure to cry.

It is said by some that Little Boy Blue was Cardinal Wolsey. Wolsey was the son of an Ipswich butcher, and as a boy, he undoubtedly looked after his father's livestock.[1] The sheep represent the English people.

Wolsey lived splendidly in his magnificent home, unmindful of the dangers ahead. In like terms, Little Boy Blue lay fast asleep unaware of the troubles all around him. He would be awakened shortly. Cardinal Wolsey was awakened to worldly tribulation when King Henry VIII dismissed him from his office.[2]

1. Opie, Iona and Peter, *The Oxford Dictionary of Nursery Rhymes,* Clarendon Press, 1951
2. Gregory, O.B., *Henry VIII,* A. Wheaton & Co., Exeter, 1977, p. 14.

PAPER TUBE HORNS
Art

Materials: paper towel or toilet paper tubes
colored masking tape
paint
waxed paper
rubber bands

Method: The teacher wraps the "mouth" end of the tube with colored masking tape. Children then paint the tube above the tape. A piece of waxed paper is placed over the opposite end and secured with a rubber band. When blown through it will vibrate.

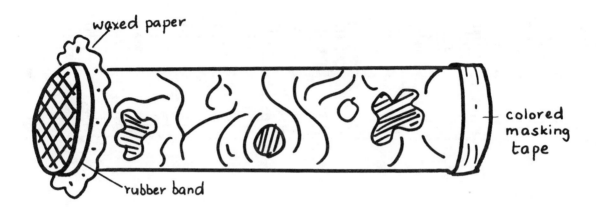

RHYMING EXERCISE
Language Arts

The teacher repeats the rhyme and the children fill in the missing word.

Little Boy *Red*
Come make your _____.

Little Boy *Yellow*
You're a jolly good _____.

Little Boy *Green*
As skinny as a _____.

Little Boy *Pink,*
Put the dishes in the _____.

Little Boy *White,*
Come say "good _____.

Little Boy *Black,*
Pat yourself on the _____.

Little Boy *Gray,*
Put your food on a _____.

Little Boy *Brown,*
Let's go to _____.

LITTLE BOY BLUE SONG
Music

Lit- tle Boy Blue, come blow your horn, The sheep's in the mead- ow, the cow's in the corn,

Where is the boy that looks af- ter the sheep? He's un- der the hay - cock, fast a- sleep.

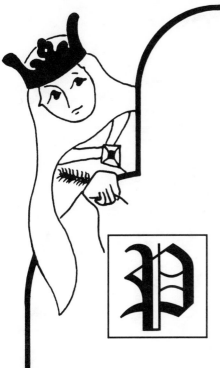

Pussy Cat, Pussy Cat

Pussy cat, Pussy cat, where have you been?
"I've been to London to visit the Queen."
Pussy cat, Pussy cat, what did you there?
"I frightened a little mouse under a chair."

The Queen in this rhyme is widely supposed to have been Elizabeth I. The tale of the pussy cat and the mouse relates to an actual incident that took place in the palace during her reign.[1]

---

1. Baring-Gould William and Ceil, *The Annotated Mother Goose,* Bramhall House, 1962, pp. 116–117.

Humanics

PRINTING CATS
Art

Materials: plastic meat trays from the grocery store
tempera paint
liquid soap
paint brushes
paper (manila or colored construction paper)

Method: The teacher cuts off the edges of the plastic meat trays. Children use either a pencil or a ball point pen to draw a cat on his or her tray.

Using tempera mixed with liquid soap, the children paint completely over the surface of their trays and then place a piece of paper on top of it and print it.

After the prints are made, the children should name their cats and have a cat art show.

CAT BOOKS
Language Arts

The teacher checks out all the cat books in the library and places them on a table in the schoolroom. Children are then free to look at them. Ultimately, someone will notice that they are all about cats. Children may request that the teacher read favorite books to the class.

MOTHER CAT AND KITTENS
Game

This game is a surefire hit with young children!

One child is selected to be the mother cat. All the other children are the kittens and they sit on the floor near her. Mother cat says, "Children, it is getting late. Get in your beds and go to sleep. Don't get up for anything. I am going to sleep, also." The child who is the mother cat hides her eyes and pretends to sleep. As soon as she hides her eyes, all the kittens quietly get up and find hiding places in the room. When they are all hidden, the teacher wakes the mother cat and tells her to find those naughty kittens. Mother cat hunts for the kittens and as each kitten is found, it returns to sit on the floor. The last kitten found is the winner and becomes the next mother cat.

Hint: Remind the children that they must not reveal another child's hiding place.

Humanics

Baa, Baa Black Sheep

Baa, baa, black sheep
Have you any wool?
Yes, sir, yes, sir,
Three bags full;
One for my master,
And one for my dame
And one for the little boy
Who cries in the lane.

When Edward VI became king of England in 1547, he was only nine years old. He was the son of Henry VIII and Jane Seymour. During his reign the demand for wool was universal. In the wool trade the division of the bags is said to refer to the export tax that was imposed on wool in 1275.[1]

"My master and my dame" symbolizes King Edward VI and the wealthy nobility. The "little boy who cries in the lane" is said to represent the common people, who always received the smallest share of the goods.[2]

1. Iona and Peter Opie, *The Oxford Dictionary of Nursery Rhymes,* Clarendon Press, 1973, p. 88.
2. Katherine Elwes Thomas, *The Real Personages of Mother Goose,* Lothrop, 1930, pp. 85, 86.

Humanics

SHEEP PUPPETS
Art

Materials: black felt
various colored yarn
buttons for eyes
hole puncher
plastic embroidery needles

various colored felt scraps
glue and white chalk
scissors
pattern of sheep's head

Method: Children are given a pattern to trace and cut out on two pieces of black felt. (White chalk may be used to trace.)
    Holes are punched by the children or the teacher around the edges of the hand puppet for stitching. Using buttons, yarn, felt scraps, glue, etc., children decorate their sheep puppets.

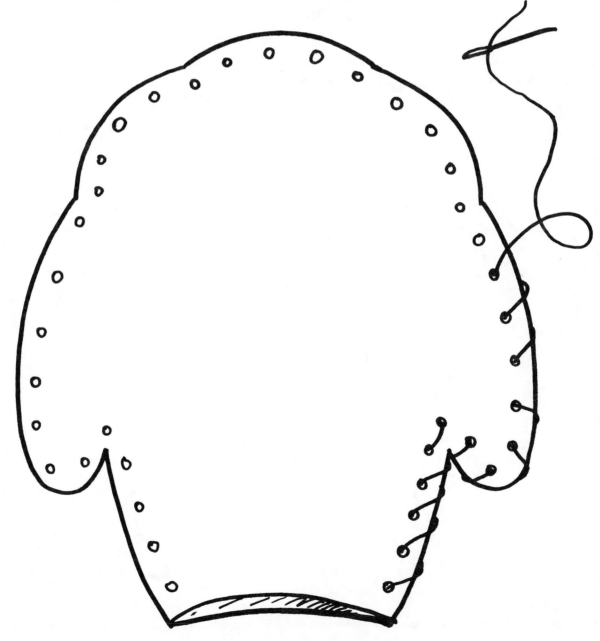

SHEEP SPONGE PAINTING
Art

Materials: sponges cut into small shapes
bowls of white tempera paint
black construction paper
stencils of sheep

Method: The child places a stencil on the center of a black piece of construction paper and sponge paints around it with white paint. When the stencil is removed, the outline of a black sheep will appear.

Humanics

PAPER WEAVING
Art

Materials: construction paper
strips of various colored paper
scissors
stapler

Method: Each child folds a 9″ × 12″ piece of paper in half (lengthwise). The teacher, using a ruler, draws a line 1½″ or 2″ from and parallel to one of the cut edges. This is the guide line. The child then cuts a series of parallel slits from the folded edge to the teacher's guiding line. (For very young children, the paper should be folded and cut in advance by the teacher.)

Children open their papers flat and weave strips of paper in and out of the slits. Each strip is begun alternately over, then under the cut paper.

Strips may be stapled before and after weaving for easier execution. Also, at least two colors of strips should be used, alternating them.

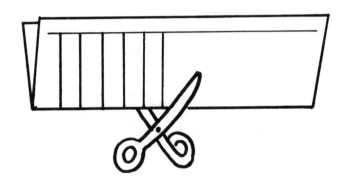
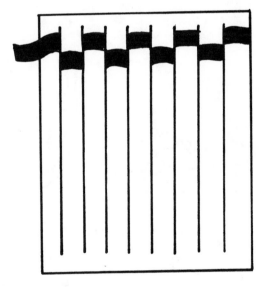

WOOL
Language Arts

General discussion about wool: Where does wool come from? How is it obtained? Which countries are sheep-raising countries? Why is wool useful? When do people wear it? Does any child own anything made of wool? Can you show it to the class today?

FULL AND EMPTY
Mathematics

Each child is handed a xerox of the "Full and Empty" worksheet, and asked to color all the bags that are full and then count them.

Color all the full bags

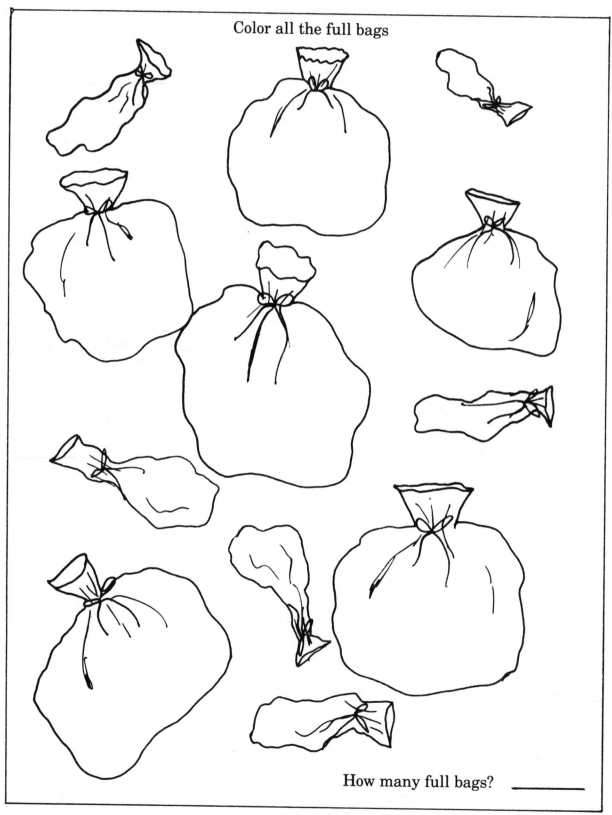

How many full bags? _____

Humanics

CHALKBOARD EXERCISE WITH 3'S
Mathematics

Discuss "3's"—triplets, tricycle, triangle, Triceratops, etc.

A large 3, written on white paper with a felt marker, is taped on the chalkboard. The teacher then writes a numeral containing a "3" on the chalkboard. Numerals such as 13, 23, 43, 53, 103, any of the 30's, etc. may be written. After it is guessed it is erased. Children try to guess the numeral. Those who guess correctly might have their names written on the board.

SELF-CONCEPTS
Social Studies

Hold a class discussion: "Why do you think the boy was crying?" "What would make you cry?" "Is it all right to cry?"

FEELY BAG
Science

The teacher collects samples of a variety of materials including wool, cotton, silk, velvet, burlap, denim, satin, etc. During a directed lesson, these samples are passed around for the children to feel. They are identified and their properties discussed.

The cloth samples are then placed in a paper bag and the teacher calls children, one at a time, to reach into the bag without looking and select a particular kind of material, i.e.: "Pick out a piece of silk."

Ride A Cock-Horse

Ride a cock-horse
To Banbury Cross,
To see a fine lady upon a white horse.
With rings on her fingers and bells on her
  toes,
She shall have music wherever she goes.

The term "cock-horse" has been used to describe a proud, high-spirited horse.[1]

K. E. Thomas states that the fine lady refers to Elizabeth I. At the beginning of her reign, many plans were carried through for restoring confidence in her subjects after the bloody rule of her sister, Mary I. One plan, a royal procession to Banbury Cross served for an historic painting.

Historians generally agree that Elizabeth was inordinately fond of rings.[2] The bells on her toes refers to a custom begun in the 15th century when a bell was worn on the long, tapering toe of each shoe.[3]

---

1. Iona and Peter Opie, *The Oxford Dictionary of Nursery Rhymes*, Clarendon Press, 1973, p. 66.
2. K. E. Thomas, *The Real Personages of Mother Goose*, Lothrop, 1930, pp. 160, 161.
3. Opie, *The Oxford Dictionary of Nursery Rhymes*, 1973, p. 66.

Humanics

FINGER PAINTED HORSES
Art

Materials: finger paint
finger paint paper
scissors
horse patterns
felt markers

Method: After children have finger painted, their papers are allowed to dry. Then, using a cardboard pattern of a horse, they trace it on their finger paint papers and cut it out. These are posted on a bulletin board.

COPY THE WORDS
Language Arts

Several 3″ × 5″ cards, each containing a printed word found in the "Ride a Cock Horse" rhyme, are placed on a table. Words such as *horse, bells, rings, lady, fingers, toes,* etc., may be used. Children are given lined paper and pencils. They copy the words on their papers.

MAZE
Art

Children are given a maze worksheet. The lady on the horse must get to Banbury Cross. Sometimes trees block the road. They are asked to color the road to Banbury Cross.

Humanics

Hey Diddle, Diddle

ey, diddle, diddle,
The cat and the fiddle,
The cow jumped over the moon.
The little dog laughed to see such sport,
And the dish ran away with the spoon.

Although this is considered to be an Elizabethan jingle, the introduction "Hey diddle, diddle" is an exceedingly ancient phrase.[1] However, it is well known that Elizabeth I was the queen who was passionately fond of dancing and of the fiddle. She often kept a fiddler playing while she spent hours dancing.[2]

It is said that she was fond of teasing her ministers just as a cat plays with a mouse. These advisors were given nicknames such as "moon" and "lap-dog." At mealtimes her food was carried in by a gentleman called "dish," and a lady-in-waiting, "spoon," always tasted her soup first. When "dish" and "spoon" eloped, this rhyme ws invented.[3]

---

1. Katherine Elwes Thomas, *The Real Personages of Mother Goose,* Lothrop, 1930, p. 136.
2. Ibid.
3. *World Book Encyclopedia,* Volume 13, 1972, p. 699.

72   *Humanics*

PAPER BAG PUPPETS
Art

Materials: small paper bags
colored construction paper
yarn, gummed circles, gummed stars, glitter, etc.
glue
scissors and stapler

Method: Children are asked to select one of the characters in the rhyme and create a puppet of that character. Each child is given a paper bag and the trimmings to decorate it as they please. Creativity is encouraged.

WHAT THEY DID
Art

Each child is asked to draw a picture of what one of the characters in the rhyme did. These are then tacked on the bulletin board in chronological order or they may be stapled into a class booklet.

WHAT IS WRONG WITH THIS PICTURE?
Language arts

If possible, reproduce the picture illustrating the rhyme and pass it out to each child during discussion time. Ask them what is wrong with the picture. The following examples of questions may be used: Have you ever seen a cat play a fiddle? What is a fiddle? Is it hard to play? Could a cow jump over the moon? Why not? Could an astronaut jump over the moon? Do little dogs laugh? Could a dish run away with a spoon?

NICKNAMES
Language Arts

Hold a discussion with the class: What is a nickname? Think of a reason why someone might be called "spoon," or "dish," etc. Does anyone in the class have a nickname? Do you know anyone with a nickname?

FIDDLE MUSIC
Music

The best demonstration of a fiddle would be to have someone (a parent) visit the class and play a fiddle for the children. If this is not possible, play two or three short selections on records. Some country "fiddlin" music could be compared to a classical violin solo.

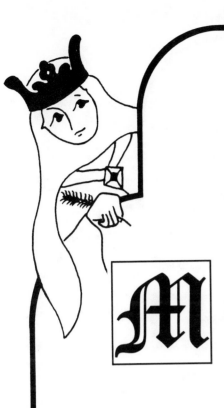

Mistress Mary

Mistress Mary,
Quite contrary,
How does your garden grow?
With silver bells and cockle shells
And fair maids all in a row.

Popular belief states that Mistress Mary was Mary, Queen of Scots. Her gay French and Popish ways displeased many, especially the fiery preacher, John Knox, who was head of the reform Church of Scotland.[1]

The pretty maids were thought to be her ladies-in-waiting, while the cockle shells referred to a particular dress of hers which was a present from the Dauphin.

---

1. Iona and Peter Opie, *The Oxford Dictionary of Nursery Rhymes*, Clarendon Press, 1973, p. 301.
2. Ibid.

Humanics

BELLS, SHELLS, AND FAIR MAID STAMPS
Art

Materials: string
glue
3 blocks of wood
paper
tempera paint and brushes
thin sponges

Method: Each block (or stamp) will contain either a shell, bell, or fair maid.
The teacher covers one side of the block with a thin coat of glue. A
piece of string is then dipped into the glue with the excess pulled off
with fingers. The string is placed on the block to form a design of either
a shell, bell, or fair maid. (String should not overlap.) Allow to dry
thoroughly.
Either paint the string with thin tempera or pour paint on a
sponge and impress the stamp first on the sponge and then on paper.
Note: A trial print on scrap-paper is recommended.

BRAINSTORMING
Language Arts

Children discuss gardens: kinds of gardens, when they bloom, what kind of
care they need, who takes care of them, etc. Then the teacher asks the children to
name all the kinds of flowers they might find in a garden. They are encouraged to
speak out quickly.

FAIR MAIDS IN A ROW
Mathematics

Using a sheet of light blue posterboard, the teacher pastes 10 flower pots in a row. Each has one to ten "fair maids" drawn on it. Laminate, then split open the tops.

The teacher draws and cuts out ten "fair-maid" flowers with long stems from posterboard. Each is numbered from one to ten. Various colored felt-tipped markers may be used to decorate the bonnets or faces of the flowers.

Children insert the numbered "fair-maid" flowers into the corresponding flowers pots.

Humanics

GROWING PLANTS
Science

Each child is given an empty can (either a juice can or a soup can). The cans are washed and then dried. They may then be covered with stamped paper (see "Bells, Shells, and Fair Maid Stamps," page 77.)

The teacher provides potting soil and each child fills his/her can with soil. Seeds which grow rapidly are purchased and each child places about a dozen seeds in his/her can. (Mustard seeds grow very fast.)

The cans are watered each day and placed in the sun. Children observe them and a chart may be used noting the first growth. Children may measure the growth of their plants with a ruler for about a week before taking them home.

FEELINGS
Social studies

A class discussion is held about feelings. Children are asked to define the word "contrary." What might make a child feel contrary? Other feelings are discussed.

A table is set up containing old magazines and scissors. Children are asked to cut out pictures of peoples' faces, especially faces that depict feelings. These are pasted on a chart tablet. The caption, "feelings" may be printed at the top of the chart tablet.

Children are then asked to describe the faces and select a name for each such as "happy," "silly," "funny," "sad," "dizzy," "contrary," etc. The names are printed under each face by the teacher.

Little Miss Muffet

Little Miss Muffet
Sat on a tuffet,
Eating her curds and whey;
There came a great spider
Who sat down beside her
And frightened Miss Muffet away.

When Mary became Queen of Scots she was only one week old. At the age of six she was sent to France to live and be educated. She returned to Scotland to rule when she was eighteen. During the time that she sat on her throne (tuffet) she encountered bitter opposition, mainly because of her Catholic religion.

K.E. Thomas states that Mary, Queen of Scots, was Little Miss Muffet and that John Knox was the spider.[1] Under the leadership of John Knox, Scotland's national religion became Presbyterian. This was only one of the tribulations that "frightened" Mary off the throne.

---

1. Katherine Elwes Thomas, *The Real Personages of Mother Goose*, Lothrop, 1930, p.p. 175, 176.

Humanics

SPIDERS
Art

Materials: cardboard apple trays (obtained from grocery stores)
scissors
paint and brushes
pipe cleaners

Method: Using cardboard apple trays, children cut out the indented "dishes." (For younger children, the teacher will do this.) Each child paints one and when it is dry, inserts four pipe cleaners around the edge for legs.

TUFFETS
Art

Materials: material cut in 14″ squares
yarn
embroidery needles
cotton stuffing

Method: Using two squares of material, the teacher pins together three sides. The child then stitches these with yarn. (It is suggested that the teacher insert the first stitch which contains a knot.) The "tuffet" is then stuffed and the fourth side is stitched. Children may use these for play and rest.
    Note: Webster's Dictionary gives one definition of a tuffet as a low seat.

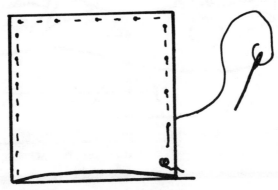

Lessons from Mother Goose

SPIDER WEBS
Mathematics

Children are given worksheets with a small square or pentagon drawn in the center. They are asked to draw increasingly larger squares (or pentagons) around it. They then draw lead lines from each corner to the center. They then draw a spider(s) on their webs.

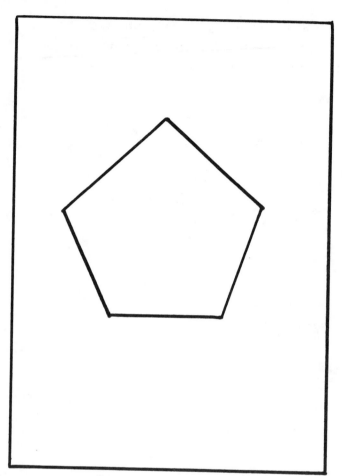

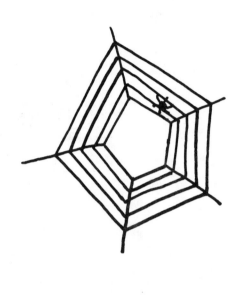

CURDS AND WHEY
Science

The teacher brings a carton of cottage cheese to school and each child is given a small portion to eat. They discuss what it is. Cottage cheese is also curds and whey. (The whey is the liquid and the curds are the lumps.)

INSECTS

Children discuss insects and arachnids. How do they differ? In some instances spiders are useful. How? (They kill other insect pests such as flies, mosquitoes, gnats, etc.)

Little Bo-Peep

ittle Bo-Peep has lost her sheep
And can't tell where to find them.
Leave them alone and they'll come home,
Wagging their tails behind them.

Little Bo-Peep fell fast asleep
And dreamt she heard them bleating;
When she awoke, she found it was a joke,
For they were still a-fleeting.

The days of open fields in the English country-side are reflected in Little Bo-Peep. Animals often strayed if their watchers fell asleep.[1] It is thought by some that Little Bo-Peep is a rhyme about Mary, Queen of Scots.

The sheep were her own clansmen who, at one time, turned against her. "Leave them alone and they'll come home" is interpreted as an admonition to Mary to forgive the rebels and bring the clans together again.[2] Nothing ever came of this.

1. Opie, Iona and Peter, *A Family Book of Nursery Rhymes,* Oxford University Press, 1964, p. 192.
2. Katherine Elwes Thomas, *The Real Personages of Mother Goose,* Lothrop 1930, p.p. 189, 190.

Humanics

SPONGE PRINT SHEEP
Art

Materials: sponges
tempera paint in empty pie tins
paper

Method: Several simple sheep-like shapes are cut out of sponges by the teacher. Children dip a sheep sponge in paint, wiping off the excess paint and printing it on their papers.

MATCHING SHEEP GAME
Language Arts

Using different patterned wallpaper, the teacher cuts out matching pairs of sheep. (The above pattern may be used.)

One set of sheep is hidden around the room, and the matching set is placed in a basket on a table. Each child is given an envelope with his or her name written on it. The envelopes are placed on the same table as the basket of sheep.

Children search the room for sheep. When a child finds one, it must be matched with its identical pattern. The child then puts the sheep into his/her envelope. When all the sheep in the basket are gone, the game is over. Whoever has the most pairs of sheep in his/her envelope, wins.

COUNTING SHEEP GAME
Language Arts

The children close their eyes and pretend to be asleep. The teacher taps a ruler several times on a desk and says, "Wake up, Little Bo-Peep, your sheep are gone. How many sheep did you lose?" The children open their eyes and tell the teacher how many sheep she lost by the number of taps they heard.

COUNT THE SHEEP WORKSHEET
Mathematics

The teacher prepares a worksheet with many sheep on it. Children are asked to count and color the sheep.

Humanics

Daffy-Down-Dilly

D affy-down-dilly has come to town
In a yellow petticoat and a green gown.

Daffy-down dilly is an expansion of the name "daffodil." It was known to be used as far back as 1573 and is still a name for the yellow daffodil in dialect form.[1]

---

1. Iona and Peter Opie, *The Oxford Dictionary of Nursery Rhymes,* Clarendon Press, 1973, p. 141.

Humanics

DAFFODILS
Art

Materials: white construction paper
pencils
circle patterns (cut from cardboard)
green and yellow paint
paint brushes
paper baking cups
glue
glitter

Method: The teacher cuts out several cardboard circles slightly larger than the bottoms of the baking cups.

Children are asked to trace several circles on their papers with a pencil—not too close together. Around the circles they paint yellow petals, green stems, and leaves.

While this is drying, children are given paper baking cups. They put glue and glitter on the inside bottoms of the cups and then glue them in each circle on their papers.

FLOWER GAME
Language Arts

The teacher obtains two similar flower catalogues from a nursery. Pairs of flowers that are the same are cut out and mounted on construction paper. If possible, laminate at this point. The flower cards are kept in a cigar box. One or two children at a time take turns matching the pairs.

IDENTIFYING PLANT PARTS
Science

Each child is given a duplicated copy of a flower. The four main parts are written across the bottom of the page. They must copy these in the proper blanks. Flowers may also be colored with crayons.

Roots   Stem   Leaves   Flower

Humanics

Ring Around A Rosie

Ring around a rosie,
A pocket full of posie,
Ashes, ashes,
We all fall down

(Variation)
Ring-a ring o'roses,
A pocket full of posies,
A-tishoo! A tishoo!
We all fall down.

It is believed that this rhyme refers to the Great Plague. The 'roses' describes the rosy rash which was one of the first symptoms, while the 'posies' were the herbs and spices which people often carried to ward off the infection.

As for the sneeze ("A tishoo"), it suggests the last symptom before falling down dead.[1]

---

1. Mulherin, Jennifer, editor, *Popular Nursery Rhymes,* Granada Publishing, 1984, pp. 110–111.

Humanics

RINGS OF ROSES HEADBANDS
Art

Materials: pipe cleaners
masking tape
stapler
crepe paper
tissue paper/construction paper for flowers
pencils
scissors
glue

Method: Children are given tissue paper petals. One petal at a time is glued around a pipe cleaner beginning at the top and working down. Staples may be used to reinforce the glue. To make headbands, the teacher twists the ends of two pipe cleaners together to form a circle. Masking tape is used to reinforce the connections. Crepe paper is twisted around the circle and secured with a staple. Attach tissue flowers to pipecleaner headband.

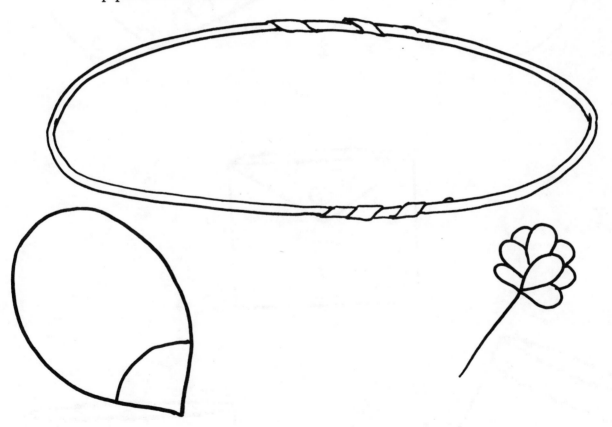

POCKET WORKSHEET
Mathematics

Give each child a "Pockets Worksheet," and ask them to draw the correct number of posies in each pocket.

POCKETS
Language Arts

Discuss what pockets are used for. Discuss other ways to carry things: pocketbooks, suitcases, paper bags, boxes, jars, baskets, etc.

Humanics

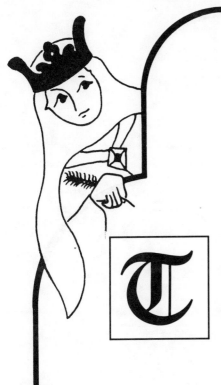

There Was An Old Woman

There was an old woman who lived in a shoe,
She had so many children she didn't know
what to do.
She gave them some broth—without any
bread;
She whipped them all soundly and sent them
to bed!

Some scholars believe that Parliament was "the old woman" who geographically lived in a shoe, which was the British Isles. She ruled over her many children—the far-flung Empire.

Parliament gave her children a bitter cup of broth in the cordially disliked person of James I of Scotland.[1]

---

1. Baring-Gould, William and Ceil, *The Annotated Mother Goose*, Bramhall House, 1962, p. 86.

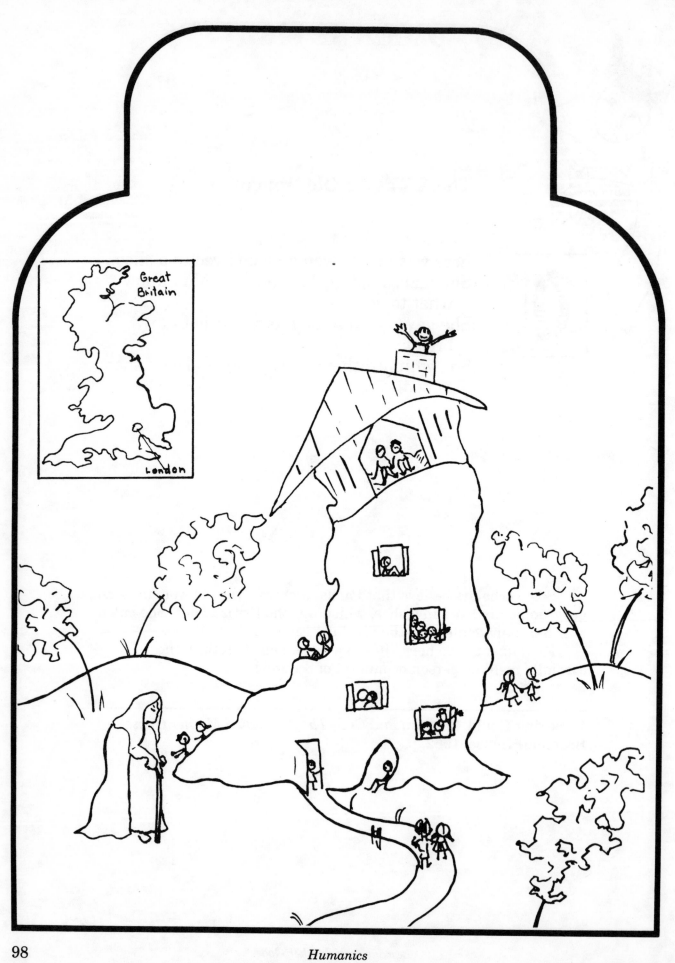

Great Britain

London

Humanics

LACE THE SHOE
Art

Materials: various colored posterboard rectangles (8½″ × 12″)
marking pens
scissors
hole puncher
shoe laces or yarn

Method: Each child traces a foot on a posterboard rectangle. They then cut them out. With teacher's assistance, holes are punched for eyelets. Using shoe laces, the children tie their own shoes. If yarn is used for lacing, it is suggested that the ends be dipped in wax or wrapped with cellophane tape.

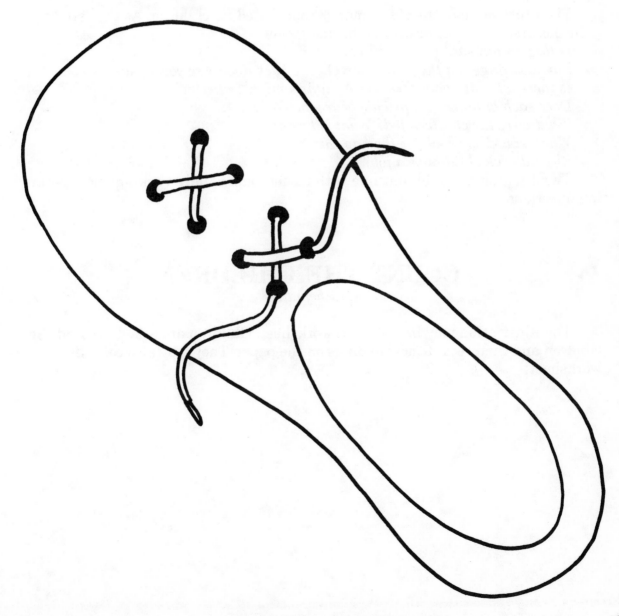

MAP PICTURES
Art

Materials: several road maps cut in rectangles (12″ × 18″) for ease in handling.
tracing paper
assorted felt markers

Method: Children are given sections of maps. They try to find designs on their maps. They place tracing paper over their maps and color in areas to form a design.

DISCUSSION
Language Arts

The illustration of the old woman is reproduced for children. As they study their pictures, the teacher begins the discussion:
Is this an unusual house? Why?
Put your finger on the front door. On the back door. Are you sure?
Is there a living room? Where? A bathroom? A bedroom?
Does each child have a private bedroom? Why not?
What were the children fed? What is broth?
What would you cook for them to eat?
Should each child have a job?
The discussion should continue with teacher and children asking and answering questions.

COUNT THE CHILDREN
Mathematics

The illustration may be used as a worksheet. Children are asked to count the children and then record their findings on the paper. They may also color the worksheet.

OPPOSITES IN NATURE
Science

Montessori introduced this kind of activity which has been adapted successfully by other systems. The teacher prepares pairs of 6″ × 8″ oak tag cards. On each pair, opposite geographical features are drawn such as: island and lake, ocean and continent, mountain and canyon, isthmus and strait, volcano and crevasse, peninsula and inlet, forest and plain, cape and bay, desert and wetland, hill and valley. The children are asked to match opposites.

Mountain

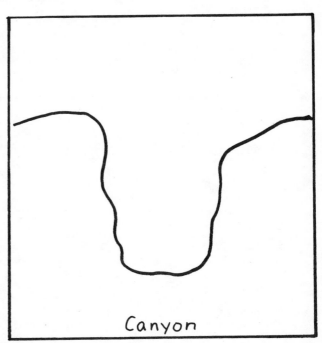

Canyon

Forest

Plain

Lessons from Mother Goose

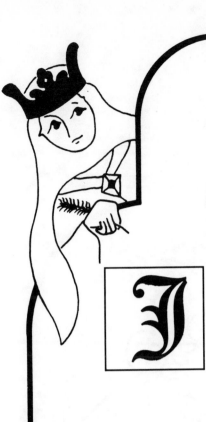

Jack Spratt

J ack Spratt could eat no fat,
His wife could eat no lean,
And so, betwixt them both, you see,
They licked the platter clean.

Katherine Elwes Thomas thought that Jack Spratt was Charles I who became king in 1625, just when Parliament was beginning to gain power.[1]

Charles demanded money from Parliament to finance a war with Spain. His wife, Henrietta Maria of France, a ruthless, grasping queen, also demanded money, but for her own personal gratification. Between them both, you see, England reeled.

---

1. Katherine Elwes Thomas, *The Real Personages of Mother Goose*, Lothrop 1930, p. 209.

FOOD PRINTING
Art

Materials: vegetables or fruit, either cut in half or sliced. The following may be used: potatoes, carrots, onions, celery, oranges, apples, etc.
tempera paint in pie tins
paper

Method: Children dip the cut side of the fruit or vegetable into the paint. The excess paint is wiped off on the edge of the pie tin. It is then pressed onto a piece of construction paper. For best results, it should be pressed on a piece of scrap paper before being printed on the construction paper.

WHAT CAN YOU MAKE FROM...?
Language Arts

The teacher suggests one kind of food such as apples. Children name all the products which can be made out of apples, such as sauce, strudel, pie, juice, cider, baked, cake, candy, etc.
Other foods might include:
grapes—juice, wine, jelly, raisins, chewing gum, jelly
strawberries—short cake, jelly, jello, ice-cream, yogurt
bananas—cake, pie, muffins, bread, bananas and milk, with cereal
potatoes—pancakes, baked, french fried, bread, mashed, boiled
carrots—cake, salad, candied

MATCHING WEIGHTED JARS
Science

The teacher collects approximately 10 opaque jars or cans. They must all be the same size. Pairs are filled with graduating amounts of sand and then they are covered tightly. (For example, one pair will be filled, another pair is ¾ filled, another ⅔ filled, etc.)

Children match the pairs by holding them in their hands and guessing which jars weigh the same. Or a balance scale may be used to find the matching pairs. As pairs are found, they may be placed on specially designed cards with circles drawn on them.

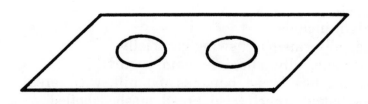

Humanics

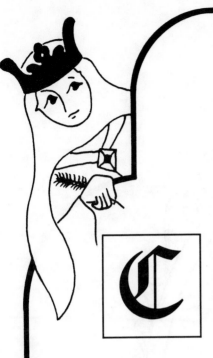

Curly Locks

Curly locks, curly locks, wilt thou be mine?
Thou shalt not wash dishes nor yet feed the
   swine,
But sit on a cushion and sew a fine seam.
And feed upon strawberries, sugar and
   cream.

Soon after Charles II was proclaimed King, Oliver Cromwell fought and defeated him in battle, and he was forced to flee. During exile in France and Holland he did many menial chores. But when the Protectorate government failed, he was recalled to the throne and he once again enjoyed all the comforts of a ruler.

Charles II was playfully called "curly locks" in his day because he introduced and wore the peruke (wig) in England.[1]

---

1. Katherine Elwes Thomas, *The Real Personages of Mother Goose,* Lothrop 1930, p. 227.

Humanics

CURLED PAPER
Art

Materials: ¼″ strips of colored construction paper
12″ × 18″ manila or white construction paper
felt marking pens or crayons
scissors
glue
large circle patterns to trace

Method: Children trace and cut out a large circle on their papers. They then draw and color a face on the circle. Using one ¼″ strip, the child twists it around a pencil and holds it tightly for a few seconds. It is then glued on the picture.

QUILLING
Art

Materials: ¼″ strips of colored construction paper
8½″ × 12″ construction paper
glue

Method: If children are capable of working with more complicated curled paper strips, the following designs may be curled and glued to paper:

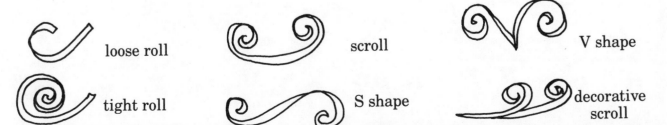

loose roll   scroll   V shape

tight roll   S shape   decorative scroll

Lessons from Mother Goose

JOBS AT HOME
Language Arts

Children discuss household jobs and are asked to think of another name for them such as "helping mother," "home jobs," "home work," etc. What household jobs did Curly Locks perform? Think of other household jobs. Do any children have jobs at home? Describe them. Name some helping jobs that might be performed at school.

HOUSEHOLD CHORES
Dramatics

One or more children take turns acting out simple tasks. The rest of the children try to guess what they are doing. Some suggestions for tasks include: cooking, sewing, washing dishes, making beds, polishing silver, setting the table, scrubbing a pot, ironing, rolling out dough, sweeping, dusting, mopping, vacuuming, etc.

PEOPLE ARE DIFFERENT
Social Studies

Children discuss people and the differences in hair such as straight, curly, wavy, thin, thick, long, short, blonde, black, brown, red, gray, uncombed, combed.

A sheet of poster board and some paste pots are placed in the center of an activity table. Children are given old magazines and scissors. They search for pictures of people with various types of hair. These are cut out and pasted randomly on the posterboard.

This collage may be discussed in a group session and the various types of hair labelled.

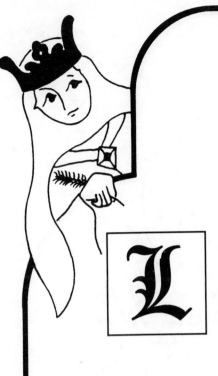

Lady Bird, Lady Bird

ady Bird, Lady Bird, fly away home.
Your house is on fire and your children are
    gone;
All except one and that's little Anne
And she has crept under the warming pan.

Queen Mary d'Este, wife of James II, is referred to as "Lady Bird."[1] She was so unpopular that she ultimately had to leave England and flee to her native France. Her husband soon followed her into exile.

One of their children, Anne, managed to remain and much later she became Queen Anne.

In the United States a Lady Bird is better known as a lady bug.

---

1. Katherine Elwes Thomas, *The Real Personages of Mother Goose*, Lothrop, 1930, pp. 281, 282.

THINGS THAT FLY
Art

Materials: long sheet of 36″ wide craft paper or brown wrapping paper for the
      mural
    various sizes of paper squares and rectangles (not too small)
    several colors of thin tempera paint
    brushes
    scissors
    glue
    fine-line marking pens

Method: The wrapping paper is taped to the wall or tacked on a bulletin board. Each square is folded in half. A few drops of paint are placed on each side. The halves are then folded together and the paint pressed.

    When opened, the "blotto" inside may resemble an insect, butterfly, or bird. Let the children decide.

    After it is dry, the painting is then outlined, cut out, and glued on the mural paper. Children make as many blottos as they desire.

    Optional: details may be marked in with the marking pen.

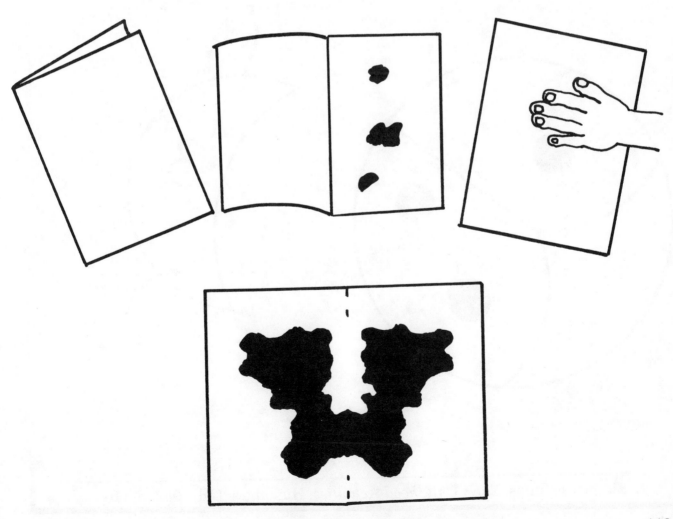

Lessons from Mother Goose

LADY BIRD DISCUSSION
Language Arts

Children look at the illustration. The teacher initiates a class discussion by asking questions such as: *Does the Lady Bird seem upset? How can you tell? Why is she upset? What would you do if your house caught on fire? What can be done to prevent fires?*

ONE TO ONE CORRESPONDENCE WITH LADYBUGS
Mathematics

The teacher cuts out eleven red posterboard circles. A different number of dots from 0 to 10 is drawn on each circle.

Eleven moon-shaped heads are drawn and cut out of posterboard. They are numbered from 0 to 10 and pipe cleaner antennae are attached to each.

The child matches each head to the body with the corresponding number of dots.[1]

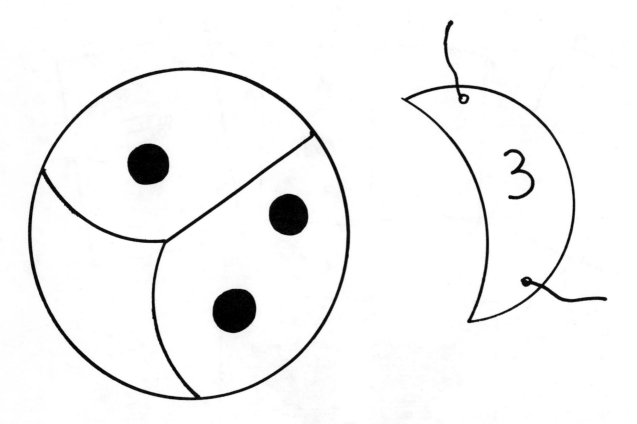

---

1. Elaine Commins, *Early Childhood Activities*, Humanics, Ltd. 1982, p. 110.

DISCUSSING BIRDS
Science

Children are asked to name some different kinds of birds. Various colors are suggested. What kind of homes do birds have? Think of sea birds and land birds. Consider the sizes of birds, from the largest (ostrich) to the smallest (hummingbird). Children are asked what they like most about birds.

In winter, have the children make bird feeders out of pine cones or empty milk cartons. They can be hung near the school or taken home.

PINE CONE BIRD FEEDER
Science

Peanut butter is inserted between the cone layers. It is then rolled in wild birdseed. The cone is then hung outside on a branch.

MILK CARTON BIRD FEEDER
Science

Children save their empty milk cartons and wash them thoroughly. The teacher cuts openings for windows and a hole is punched in the "roof" to insert a string. Crumbled bread, peanut butter, or bird seed is placed inside the cartons, and they are hung outdoors on branches.

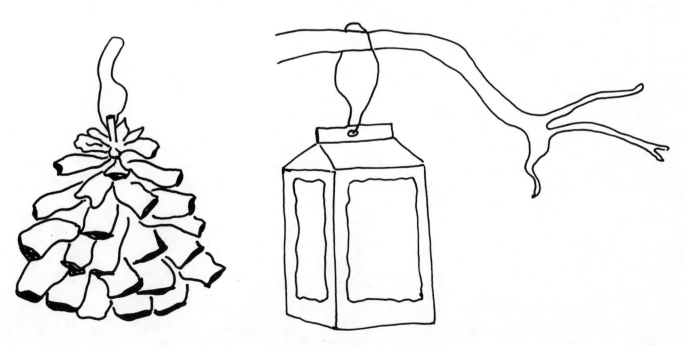

Lessons from Mother Goose

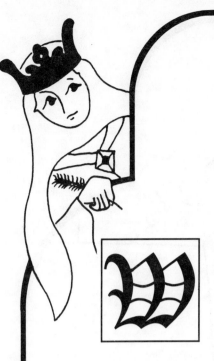

Wee Willie Winkie

ee Willie Winkie runs through the town,
Upstairs and downstairs in his nightgown;
Rapping at the window, crying through the
   lock,
"Are the children in their beds, for it's past
   eight o'clock?"

At the invitation of the leading nobles and clergymen, William of Orange was asked to return to England and rule when his father-in-law, James II, was banished.

He arrived with an army to "defend freedom and uphold the Church of England."[1] Within a week, the Jacobite Minstrelsy openly nicknamed him "Wee Willie Winkie."[2]

---

1. Katherine Elwes Thomas, *The Real Personages of Mother Goose,* Lothrop, 1930, p. 293.
2. Ibid.

Humanics

RUNNING THROUGH THE TOWN
Art

Materials: 12″ × 18″ manila or white paper
felt marking pens (dark colors)
crayons

Method: Each child is given a piece of paper and a felt marking pen. They are asked to pretend that their marking pens are Wee Willie Winkie. They let their pens "run" over the paper until a design appears. It is then colored in with crayons.[1]

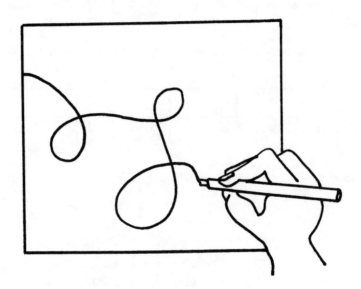

CLASS DISCUSSION
Language Arts

Why does Wee Willie Winkie rap and cry?
How can you get someone's attention?
How does a baby get someone's attention?
How does a football or basketball referee get attention?
How does a dog get someone's attention? A cat?
How does a policeman get someone's attention?
How does a fire engine get someone's attention?
How does a driver of a car or bus get someone's attention?
How does a telephone get your attention?
How does your mother (or father, etc.) get your attention?
How do people on boats get attention?
How does your teacher get your attention?
Can a plant get your attention? How?

---

1. Elaine Commins, *Early Childhood Activities*, Humanics, Ltd. 1982, p. 5.

LISTEN TO YOUR FINGERS GO RAP, RAP, RAP.
Music

As the children sing, they also act out the words of this finger play song.
Listen to your fingers go rap, rap, rap. Listen to your hands go clap, clap, clap.
Listen to your feet go tap, tap, tap. Listen to your fingers go snap, snap, snap.

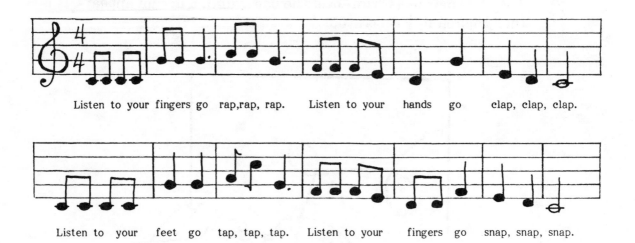

WAY TO GO
Physical Education

The teacher recites the first line of the rhyme and asks the children to run "through the town" (around the room). Children are then asked to suggest other ways Wee Willie Winkie might go through the town, i.e. Wee Willie Winkie *hops* through the town. Children then hop around the room.

BEDTIME CHART
Social Studies

The teacher prepares a chart with four or five columns. It is posted on the bulletin board. Each column is headed with a specific bedtime. Children sign their names in the appropriate column.

7:30	8:00	8:30	9:00

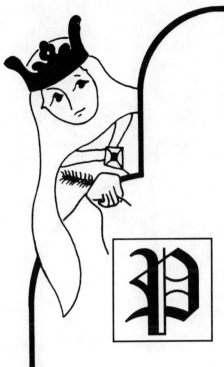

Pat-A-Cake

Pat-a-cake, pat-a-cake, baker's man
Bake me a cake as fast as you can.
Pat it and prick it, and mark it with a T,
And put it in the oven for Tommy and me.

This nursery rhyme has been known as early as 1698 as a hand clapping game to be used with very young children. It was also used as a hand-warming activity.[1]

---

1. Mulherin, Jennifer, editor, *Popular Nursery Rhymes,* Granada Publishing, 1984, p. 128.

124   *Humanics*

"AT WORDS"
Language Arts

The teacher prints about 20 "at" words on the chalkboard. A "p" is placed before the first "at" word. The children say the word "pat" together, sounding out the "p." They are then asked to think of other words that rhyme with "at," such as *fat* and *cat*. The teacher prints the appropriate letters before each "at" as each rhyming word is called out.

OTHER NURSERY RHYMES
Language Arts

When not focusing on royalty, most nursery rhymes are concerned with food, as is "Pat-A Cake." Two of these include:

> *Hot cross buns! Hot cross buns!*
> *One a penny, two a penny, hot cross buns!*
> *If you have no daughters, give them to your sons.*
> *One a penny, two a penny, hot cross buns!*
> *But if you have none of these little elves,*
> *Then you may eat them all yourselves.*

Hot Cross buns is an old street cry that was probably introduced into Britain by the Romans.[1]

> *Simple Simon met a pieman going to the fair;*
> *Said Simple Simon to the pieman, "Let me taste your ware."*
>
> *Said the pieman to Simple Simon, "Show me first your penny."*
> *Said Simple Simon to the pieman, "Indeed, I have not any."*

Scholars believe that "Simple Simon" meant a "natural silly fellow," and probably dates back to Elizabethan times.[2]

---

1. Mulherin, Jennifer, editor, *Popular Nursery Rhymes*, Granada Publishing, 1984, p. 38.
2. Ibid, p. 90.

RHYTHM
Music

Sing and play the "Pat-a-Cake" rhyme. Children may either clap hands to the beat, or pairs of children clap hands to thighs, next to hands, then to partner's hands and back to thighs. Repeat.

Another hand-clapping rhyme:

> *Peas porridge hot,*
> *Peas porridge cold,*
> *Peas porridge in the pot*
> *Nine days old.*
>
> *Some like it hot,*
> *Some like it cold,*
> *Some like it in the pot*
> *Nine days old.*

MUFFIN MAN
Music

One child is blindfolded and sits in a chair in the center of a circle. All the children walk around and sing, "Do you know the muffin man?" When the song ends, the teacher points to one child to be the muffin man. He or she walks to "it," who tries to identify him by feeling his face.[1]

OCCUPATIONS
Social Studies

Hold a class discussion of various occupations related to baking: Who makes cakes? Where can you buy them? Who serves them? From where do we get flour? Eggs? Etc.

---

1. Commins, Elaine, Early Childhood Activities, Humanics, Ltd., P.O. Box 7447, Atlanta, Georgia 30309, 1982, p. 82.

Hark, Hark

Hark, hark,
The dogs do bark,
The beggars are coming to town;
Some in rags,
And some in tags,
And one in a velvet gown.

When George I became king in 1714 there was much opposition from the Jacobite political party. They felt that George, as a German, had no right to rule in England. This is one of the rhymes they made up to ridicule him and his retinue.[1]

---

1. *The World Book Encyclopedia,* Volume 14, 1972, p. 457.

Humanics

DOG SHOW
Art

Materials: white construction paper
pencils
felt marking pens
felt scrap material
scissors
glue

Method: Children are given the materials. They are asked to draw their dogs with pencil first. Details may be colored in with marking pens and/ or felt materials may be cut to fit the drawing and then glued on the picture. (To enhance the appearance of pictures, the dogs should be mounted on colored construction paper before posting on the bulletin board.)

KINDS OF DOGS
Language arts

Pet dogs versus working dogs are considered. Children are asked to name various kinds of dogs and decide if they are pets or working dogs. Pet dogs might encompass various breeds such as spitz, shepherd, cocker-spaniels, terriers, poodles, etc. Working dogs might include guide dogs, watch dogs, police dogs, Eskimo sled dogs, St. Bernard rescue dogs, etc.

DRAW SPOTS ON THE DOG
Mathematics

The worksheet is divided into several squares. A dog is drawn in each square. A number is placed under each dog. Depending on the developmental level of the children, the numbers can range from 0–10. Children draw the corresponding number of dots on the dogs (see worksheet).

Georgie Porgie

Georgie Porgie, pudding and pie,
Kissed the girls and made them cry;
When the boys came out to play,
Georgie Porgie ran away.

Many scholars believe that this rhyme describes the behavior of George I toward the ladies in his court.[1]

---

1. *The World Book Encyclopedia,* Volume 14, 1972, p. 457.

CANDY KISS BINGO
Language Arts

Sectioned name cards are made for each child. A bowl of candy kisses is placed on each table. As letters are called by the teacher or a student, the child with a matching letter on his/her card covers it with a candy kiss. The first to cover his/her name wins. Winners may keep their kisses. At the end of play, the remaining kisses may be divided among non-winners.

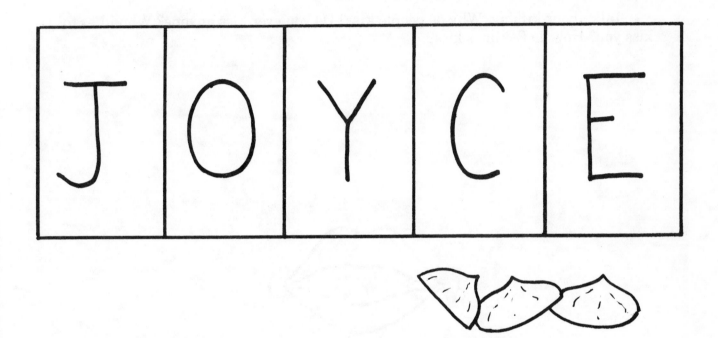

NAME RHYMES
Language Arts

Each child takes a turn saying his/her name with a nonsense rhyme similar to "Georgie Porgie," i.e., *Jackie Wachie, Laney Raney, Jodi Godie, Sammy Lammy,* etc.

PUDDING PIE
Science

Under teacher supervision, a pre-baked pie shell is filled with instant pudding. It is then refrigerated. Just before serving, the children decorate it with fresh fruit or whipped topping.

STORYTIME
Social Studies

Read "Snow White and the Seven Dwarfs" to the class. Discuss the magic kiss.

KISSING DISCUSSION
Social Studies

Talk about kissing. Why do people kiss? Do you ever kiss anyone? Who likes to kiss you? How do Eskimos kiss?

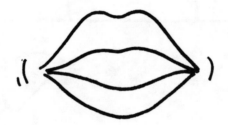

Humanics

Polly, Put The Kettle On

Polly, put the kettle on,
Polly, put the kettle on,
Polly, put the kettle on,
We'll all have tea.

Sukey, take it off again,
Sukey, take it off again,
Sukey, take it off again,
They've all gone away.

This nursery rhyme has been known since the late eighteenth century. Polly and Sukey were nicknames for Mary and Susan. Charles Dickens quotes the rhyme in one of his books.[1]

---

1. Mulherin, Jennifer, editor, *Popular Nursery Rhymes*, Granada Publishing, 1984, p. 58.

TEA TIME
Science

Discuss tea with the children: *How is tea made? Where does it come from? Where is it grown?* Children are shown crushed tea leaves, tea bags, and instant tea. Using small cups, each child may taste weak tea before and after adding sugar, ice, and/or lemon.

TEA COOKIES
Cooking

Help the children bake tea cookies in preparation for a tea party. The following recipe is easy to prepare.

Ingredients: a cake mix (any flavor)
2 eggs
2 Tablespoons of margarine
2 Tablespoons of water (for crisp cookies), 4 Tablespoons (for soft cookies)

Mix all ingredients together into a ball and refrigerate for at least ½ hour. Give each child a small amount to roll into a small ball and flatten. Bake on a cookie sheet for 10 minutes at 375 degrees.

PLACEMATS
Social Studies

The placemat pattern on the following page is duplicated for each child. Children color their "placemats." Then, using them at the table, they place toy dishes and utensils on their matching outlines. This is helpful in teaching children the proper placement of plates, cups, and utensils at the table.

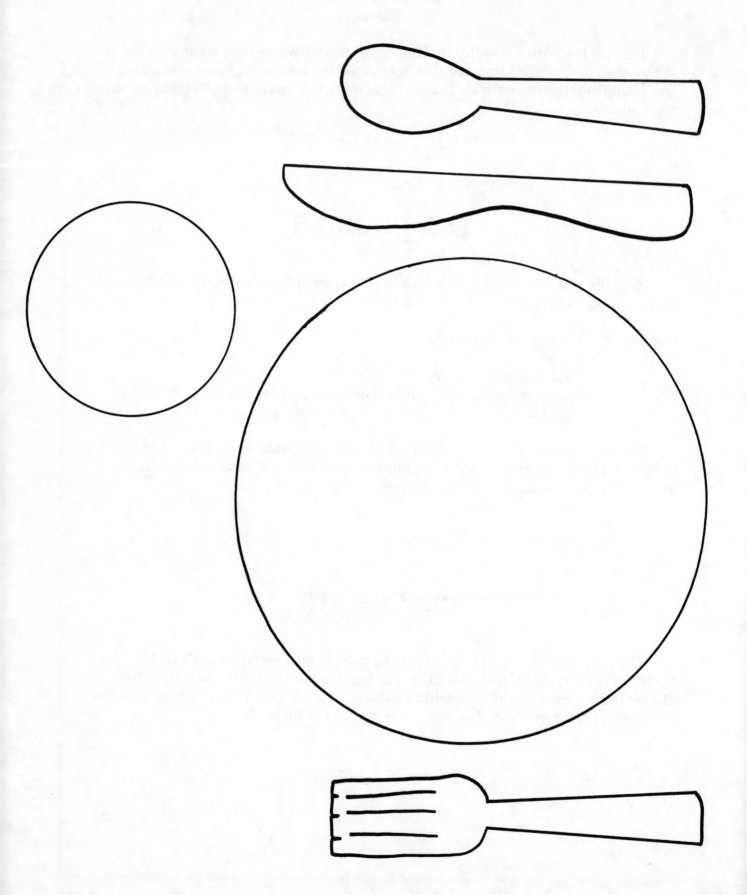

Hickory, Dickory, Dock

Hickory, dickory, dock,
The mouse ran up the clock.
The clock struck one;
The mouse ran down,
Hickory, dickory, dock.

As stated in "Blackwood's Magazine" in 1821, "Hickory, Dickory, Dock" is a counting-out rhyme frequently used by children in Edinburgh. The writer says that as far back as "could be remembered" it was chanted to decide who was to begin a game.[1]

There is a tradition in England that some of these counting-out rhymes are relics of formulas used by the Druids in choosing human sacrifices.[2]

---

1. Iona and Peter Opie, *The Oxford Dictionary of Nursery Rhymes,* Clarendon Press, 1973, p. 206.
2. William and Ceil Baring-Gould, *The Annotated Mother Goose,* Bramhall House, 1962, p. 31.

CLAY MOUSE
Art

Materials: clay, approximately 1 lb. per child
posterboard ears or patterns to trace ears
pipe cleaners
nails—preferably with gold heads
red paint

Method: Children roll their pound of clay into a flat-bottomed oval. The nose of the mouse is pinched into a point.

The teacher cuts two slits on the side of each mouse for the ears, which will be glued on after the clay dries. A pipe cleaner is inserted into each mouse for a tail, and two nails are inserted for eyes.

The mice should dry in the sun for approximately one week. If a kiln is available, the mice bodies, without eyes and tail, may be baked after drying.

When dry, a red dot is painted on the nose and, using glue, the ears are attached.

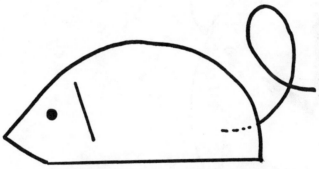

1. Make slits in wet clay and insert nails and tail

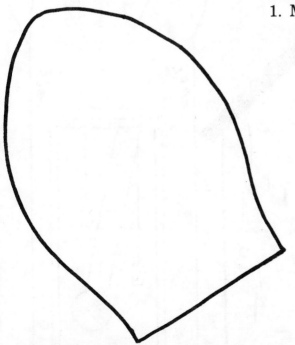

2. Children trace ear patterns on posterboard

3. Ears are glued in place and a red nose is painted on face.

PAPER PLATE CLOCKS
Art

Materials: paper plates
black construction paper hands (short and long)
brad fasteners
felt markers
cardboard clocks as models to copy

Method: Several clock models are placed on the art table. Each child is given a paper plate. With the teacher's assistance, the child places the *12, 3, 6,* and *9* in their proper positions on the clock. The children draw in the remaining hours by observing the models. Hands are bradded in last.
Optional: Clocks may be decorated with colored felt marking pens.

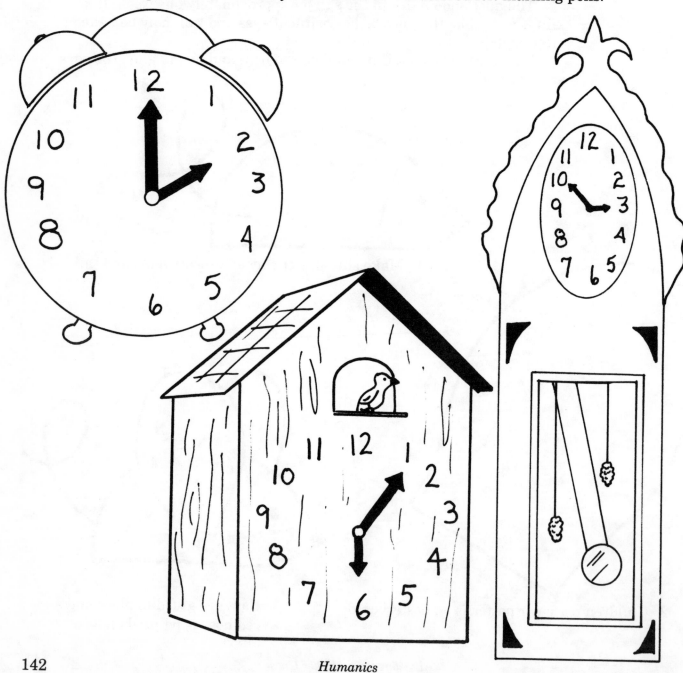

Humanics

COUNTING OUT
Language Arts

The children sit in a circle and each places one fist in front of him/her. The teacher, or a child, hits each fist while repeating the rhyme and walking around the circle. Children are also asked to repeat the rhyme. At the end of the rhyme, the last fist that is hit indicates that that child is out. Thus a child is eliminated each time the rhyme is repeated. The last child to be counted out wins.

Children are asked to think of another counting out rhymne. *(One potato, two potato, three potato, four. . . .)*

CLOCK WORKSHEETS
Mathematics

A copy of the "clock worksheet" is made for each child. Before passing out worksheets to the children, the teacher fills in the "o'clock" lines with a time. (Open time slots allow for greater individualization and variety in worksheets.) When working with younger children, the teacher should draw the minute hand on the clock faces in advance.

After the worksheets have been passed out, the children draw the hands on each clock to correspond with the time indicated below the clock face.

See page 144 for Pattern

LITTLE MOUSE, WHAT TIME IS IT?
Physical Education

One child is chosen to be the little mouse. The child walks around the playground followed by the rest of the class. The children ask the mouse, "Little mouse, what time is it?"

The mouse answers by saying, "It is two o'clock" or "It is twelve o'clock." etc.

If the mouse says, "It is one o'clock" all the children run away and the mouse must catch someone. Whoever is caught becomes the next mouse and the game begins again.

RHYMING
Language Arts

In a group session, say the rhyme, adding the hours with each verse. Have children suggest what the mouse might do.

Hickory, dickory dock, the mouse ran up the clock
The clock struck *one*, the mouse ran down
Hickory, dickory dock.

Hickory, dickory dock, the mouse ran up the clock.
The clock struck *two*, the mouse said, _____ *("Boo!")*
Hickory, dickory dock

Hickory, dickory dock, the mouse ran up the clock.
The clock struck three, the mouse said, _____ *("Whee!")*
Hickory, dickory dock

Hickory, dickory dock, the mouse ran up the clock.
The clock struck *four,* the mouse did _____ *(Roar.)*
Hickory, dickory dock.

Hickory, dickory dock, the mouse ran up the clock.
The clock struck *five,* the mouse began to _____ *(jive.)*
Hickory, dickory dock

Hickory, dickory dock, the mouse ran up the clock.
The clock struck *six,* the mouse did _____ *(Tricks.)*
Hickory, dickory dock.

Hickory, dickory dock, the mouse ran up the clock.
The clock struck *seven,* the mouse looked at _____ *(heaven.)*
Hickory, dickory dock.

Hickory, dickory dock, the mouse ran up the clock.
The clock struck *eight,* the mouse was _____ *(late.)*
Hickory, dickory dock.

Hickory, dickory dock, the mouse ran up the clock.
The clock struck *nine,* the mouse felt _____ *(fine.)*
Hickory, dickory dock.

Hickory, dickory dock, the mouse ran up the clock.
The clock struck *ten,* the mouse kissed a _____ *(hen.)*
Hickory, dickory dock.

Hickory, dickory dock, the mouse ran up the clock.
The clock struck eleven, the mouse ran back to _____ *(seven.)*
Hickory, dickory dock.

Hickory, dickory dock, the mouse ran up the clock.
The clock struck *twelve,* the mouse rang a _____ *(bell.)*
Hickory, dickory dock.

See-Saw, Margery Daw

See-saw, Margery Daw
Jack shall have a new master;
He shall have but a penny a day,
Because he can't work any faster.

Included in *Mother Goose's Melody,* 1765, See-Saw, Margery Daw is said to be sung by sawyers using two-handled saws to keep the rhythm.[1]

"Margery Daw" is an old English and Scotch term meaning idle vanity. This rhyme vaguely refers to one William Cicil who was enticed away from his studies to play cards.[2]

1. Iona and Peter Opie, *The Oxford Dictionary of Nursery Rhymes,* Clarendon Press, 1973, p. 297.
2. Katherine Elwes Thomas, *The Real Personages of Mother Goose,* Lothrop 1930, pp. 165, 166.

Humanics

ADDITION TREE
Mathematics

The teacher prepares several posterboard cards (8½ × 12) with green felt trees. At the bottom of each tree trunk is an addition problem with a blank white felt square for the answer. A collection of various colored felt leaves are placed near the felt tree cards along with many felt numerals.

Children place the number of colored leaves on the trees as is indicated in the problem. It is suggested that children use different colored leaves for each of the numbers in the problem. In this instance, they might use four yellow leaves and two red leaves. After placing the leaves on the tree, they would count them and then place a felt numeral 6 in the answer square.

See page 150 for Pattern

BALANCING ACTIVITIES
Physical Education

Children usually associate this nursery rhyme with a see-saw. Discussing the idea of balance is appropriate. Use of a balance beam in the classroom could include the following activities:

forward walk, backward walk, sideward cross-step, walk across beam with beanbag on head, sideward slide-step.

BALANCE SCALE COMPARISONS
Science

Eggs: 2 eggs are weighed while children observe. One is then hard-boiled and the eggs weighed again. What happened?

Play Dough: two equal portions of play dough are weighed. Then one is rolled into a ball while the other portion is rolled into a cylinder. Children guess which weighs most. They are weighed again. What happened?

Sponges: two equal sized sponges are weighed. One is then immersed in water. The sponges are weighed again. What happened?

Children are asked to walk around the room and select two small objects that they think might be of equal weight. They then take turns weighing their objects before the class.

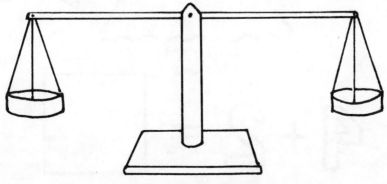

Lessons from Mother Goose

4 + 2 = ☐

TWINKLE, TWINKLE, LITTLE STAR

T winkle, twinkle little star,
How I wonder what you are;
Up above the world so high,
Like a diamond in the sky.

When the sun has gone to rest,
When he sinks down in the West,
Then you show your little light,
Twinkle, twinkle all the night.

Originally titled "The Star," this nursery rhyme first appeared in *Rhymes for the Nursery* in 1806. It was written by Jane Taylor and, although not considered a classical Mother Goose rhyme, it is one of the best known poems in the English language.[1]

---

1. Iona and Peter Opie, *The Oxford Dictionary of Nursery Rhymes*, Clarendon Press, 1973, p. 397–398.

DRAWING STARS
Art

Materials: white construction paper
pencils or felt markers
crayons

Method: Using their pencils, the children draw many capital "A's" on their construction paper. The teacher then demonstrates how stars can be made from this letter. Children may color their stars with crayons

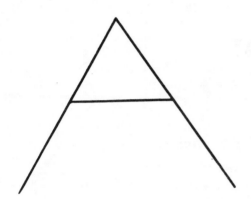 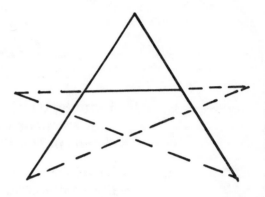

GLITTERED STARS
Art

Materials: colored construction paper
glue
glitter (silver or gold)
star templates

Method: The child places a template on his/her paper and completely fills in the star-opening with glue. Glitter is then poured on the glue. After the glitter is shaken off, a perfect star should emerge. This makes an impressive Christmas card.

FIND THE STAR GAME
Art

A glittered, posterboard star is used. All sit in a circle. One child is chosen to leave the room. The teacher then places the star in a child's lap, out of sight. No one tells who has it.

The person who is "it" returns. All begin to clap. As "it" approaches the child who has the star, the clapping gets louder. As "it" moves away from the child who has the star, the clapping gets softer.

When the person with the star is found, he/she is the next "it."

FINGER PLAY
Language Arts

Twinkle, twinkle little star
How I wonder what you are
(hands in front, open and close fingers rapidly)

Up above the world so high
Like a diamond in the sky
(arms in circle over heads)

Twinkle, twinkle little star
How I wonder what you are
(repeat first action)

STAR POEMS
Language Arts

Children are asked to write their own star poems. To enhance the activity, each child is given a duplicated sheet with a star and several blank lines on which to write a poem.

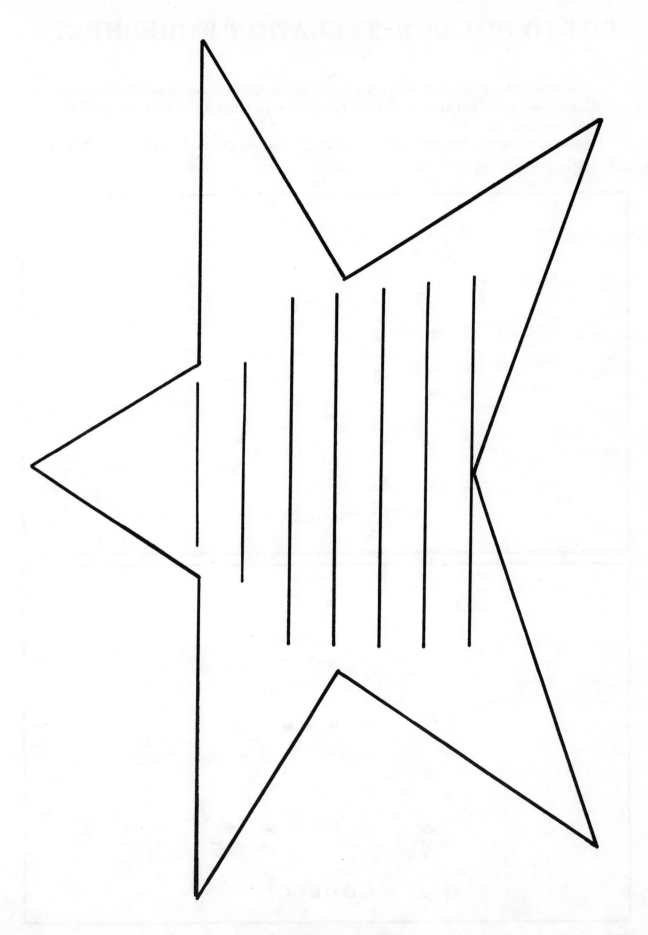

DOT-TO-DOT CONSTELLATION WORKSHEETS
Mathematics

The teacher prepares several numbered dot-to-dot constellation worksheets. Children draw lines between the numerals and copy the name of the constellation on their worksheets.

Several different constellation worksheets may be stapled together to form a booklet.

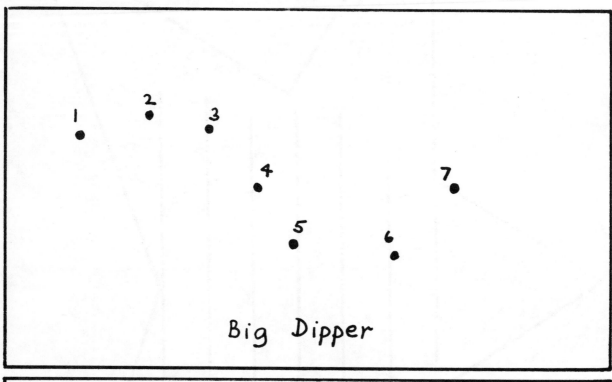

Humanics

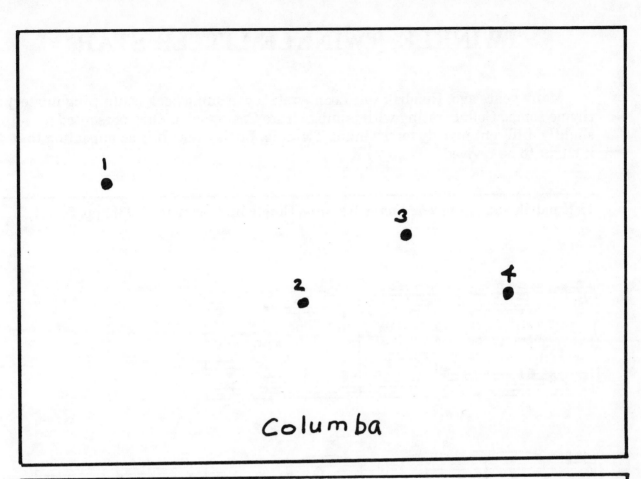

Columba

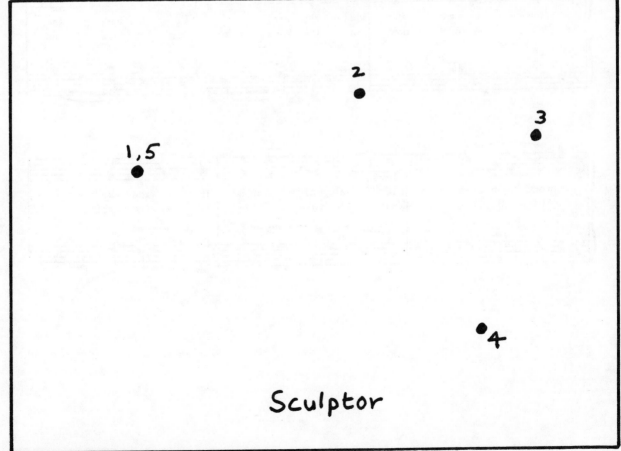

Sculptor

TWINKLE, TWINKLE LITTLE STAR
Music

Many years ago, Hendrik van Loon wrote a charming book containing nursery rhyme songs. Collaborating with pianist Grace Castagnetta, they presented a slightly different melody for Twinkle, Twinkle, Little Star.[1] It is so appealing that it ought to be revived.

---

1. Hendrik van Loon, *The Songs We Sing,* Simon and Schuster, 1936, pp. 60–61.

Humanics

STARS AND PLANETS
Science

Children discuss stars and planets. They are asked to name our closest star (Sol). They are then asked to have their parents take them outdoors on the next clear evening to observe the stars.

NIGHT AND DAY EARTH

Children are given papers containing a drawing of the Earth. It is divided in half by a line. They are asked to color half of the Earth as it would look in daytime and the other half as it would look in nighttime.

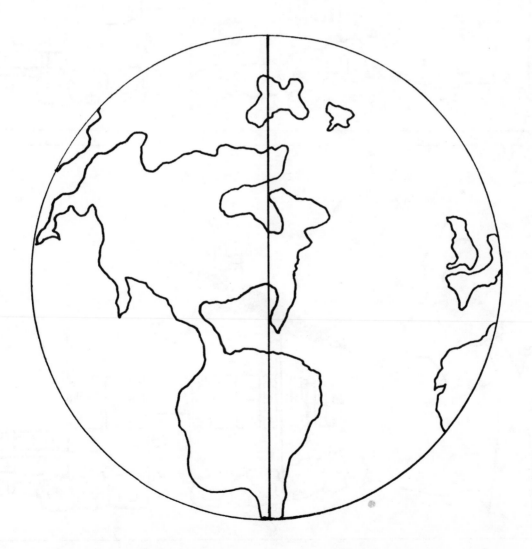

NIGHT AND DAY PICTURES

Art

Children are given papers containing two drawings. One is to be colored a daytime picture and the other to be colored a nighttime picture.

Humanics

Peter, Peter Pumpkin-Eater

Peter, Peter, pumpkin-eater
Had a wife and couldn't keep her;
He put her in a pumpkin shell,
And there he kept her very well.

Peter, Peter, pumpkin-eater,
Had another and didn't love her;
Peter learned to read and spell,
And then he loved her very well.

"Peter, Peter Pumpkin-eater" seems to have more recent origins than most of the nursery rhymes in this volume. It was first published in *Mother Goose's Quarto* in 1825 and, later, in *Aberdeen and Its Folk* in 1868.[1]

The pumpkin was thought to be a mystical vegetable. This quality is apparent in Cinderella's coach and as a Jack-O-Lantern.[2] In some countries, serf children wore a chunk of cooked pumpkin on a string around their necks to eat during the day.

---

1. Iona and Peter Opie, *The Oxford Dictionary of Nursery Rhymes*, Clarendom Press, 1973, pp. 346–347.
2. William and Ceil Baring-Gould, *The Annotated Mother Goose*, Bramhall House, 1962, pp. 127.

Humanics

FELT BOARD PUMPKIN

Art

Materials: orange felt
black felt
scissors

glue
sheet of posterboard (black)

Method: Using a large piece of orange felt, the teacher cuts out a pumpkin and glues it to a piece of posterboard. Several shapes for eyes, noses, and mouths are also cut out of the black felt. Children take turns arranging the facial features on the Jack-O-Lantern. If children are able, they may each make their own felt pumpkins and facial features.

Humanics

FINGER PLAY
Language Arts

Five little pumpkins sitting on a gate
The first one said, "My, it's getting late."
The second one said, "There are witches in the air."
The third one said, "We don't care."
The fourth one said, "Let's run, let's run."
The fifth one said, "Isn't Hallowe'en fun?"
"Oooooh!" went the wind, out went the light.
And the five little pumpkins ran out of sight.

ADDITION WORKSHEET
Mathematics

A worksheet is prepared with five or six rows of pumpkin equations. The child fills in the answer with the correct number. For example:

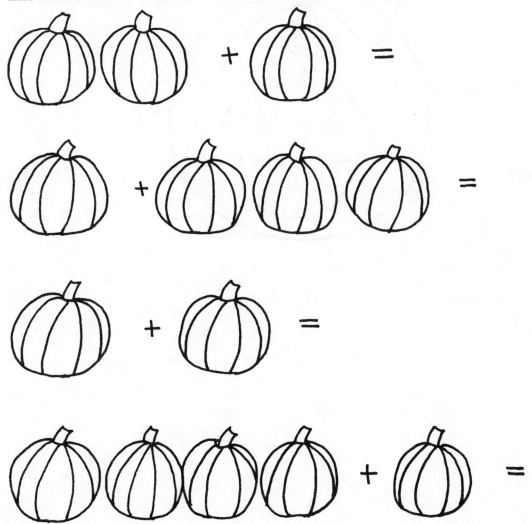

FIRE NEEDS AIR
Science

The teacher cuts off the top of a pumpkin and scoops out the insides. Before carving out a mouth and eyes, a candle is placed in the pumpkin and it is lit. The top is then replaced. What happens to the candle? Children observe that the flame has gone out.

The teacher now carves eyes and a mouth. The candle is placed inside once again, lit, and the top set back on the pumpkin. The candle will now burn. Why?[1]

---

1. Elaine Commins, *Early Childhood Activities*, Humanics Ltd. 1982, p. 225.

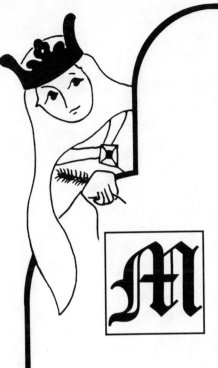

Mary Had A Little Lamb

Mary had a little lamb,
Its fleece was white as snow;
And everywhere that Mary went
The lamb was sure to go.

He followed her to school one day,
Which was against the rule;
It made the children laugh and play
To see a lamb at school.

"Mary Had a Little Lamb" was written by Sarah Joseph Hale in 1830. It is about a "partly true" incident.[1]

Considered to be a favorite by children, it is usually included in nursery rhyme anthologies.

---

1. Iona and Peter Opie, *The Oxford Dictionary of Nursery Rhymes,* Clarendon Press, 1973, p. 300.

168   *Humanics*

PICTURE PUZZLE
Art

Materials: duplicates of "Mary Had a Little Lamb" illustration
black felt-tipped marker
crayons

Method: Each child is given a copy of the "Mary Had a Little Lamb" illustration to color. When complete, the child uses a felt marker to draw in puzzle areas on the illustration. (Teachers may assist.) The child then cuts out the indicated areas.

The puzzle is now ready to assemble. Each child's puzzle parts may be kept in an envelope.

SENTENCE STRIPS
Language Arts

Sentence strips are made for each of the four lines of the first verse of the rhyme. Individual cards are made to cover each word. (For ease in identification, these individual word cards should be a different color. The child takes a strip and covers the words with its matching word card.

ANIMAL BABIES
Language Arts

Children are asked to think of different animals and what their babies are called. Examples are: sheep, lamb; horse, colt; cow, calf; dog, puppy; cat, kitten; seal, seal pup; duck, duckling; deer, fawn; cicada, nymph; lion, cub; pig, piglet.

LAMB'S COTTONBALL GAME
Mathematics

Children are given patterns of a lamb to trace and cut out of colored construction paper.

Using their lambs, a die, a package of cotton balls, and glue, one player begins by rolling the die (up to four players may play at a time). He/she glues the number of cotton balls on his/her lamb corresponding to the number on the die. The first to cover the lamb with cotton balls wins.

Humanics

Peter Piper

eter Piper picked a peck of pickled peppers;
A peck of pickled peppers Peter Piper picked;
If Peter Piper picked a peck of pickled
   peppers,
Where's the peck of pickled peppers Peter
   picked?

This tongue twister first appeared in print in 1815. It was popularly believed that if repeated three times in one breath, it would cure hiccups.[1]

---

1. Mutherin, Jennifer, editor, *Popular Nursery Rhymes*, Granada Publishing, 1984, p. 137.

Humanics

A PECK OF PICKLES BULLETIN BOARD
Art and Mathematics

Materials: green construction paper
pencils
scissors

Method: The teacher posts drawing of eight large jars, labelled "quarts," on the bulletin board. Children are given paper, pencils, and scissors. They are asked to fill the jars with pickles that they draw and cut out (jars are "filled" by tacking pickles on jars). The bulletin board is complete when all eight jars are filled. *Note:* eight quarts equals one peck.

TONGUE TWISTERS
Language Arts

The teacher asks the class to think of other tongue twisters. The following are a few examples:

A big blue bucket of blue blueberries.

How much wood would a woodchuck chuck
If a woodchuck could chuck wood?
He would chuck, he would, as much as he could
If a woodchuck could chuck wood.

She sells seashells by the seashore.

HOW MANY "P"'S?
Mathematics

The teacher prints the rhyme *"Peter Piper"* on the chalkboard in large letters. Children count all the "p's" that they can find. Each child's guess is recorded. When all have guessed, then the class counts together to find the correct answer.

HICCUPS
Science

Children discuss hiccups. Why do people get them? They are then asked to suggest cures. A homework assignment is given and children are asked to have parents and grandparents give them old-time remedies. A class discussion is held, and all who volunteer can give the answer.

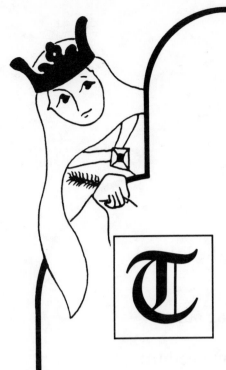

Three Little Kittens

Three little kittens, they lost their mittens,
And they began to cry,
"Oh, Mother dear, we sadly fear
Our mittens we have lost."
"What! Lost your mittens, you naughty
    kittens!
Then you shall have no pie."
"Meeow, meeow, meeow.
Then you shall have no pie."

The three little kittens they found their
    mittens,
And they began to cry.
"Oh, Mother dear, see here, see here,
Our mittens we have found."
"What! found your mittens, you good little
    kittens,
Then you shall have some pie.
Purrr, purrr, purrr,
You shall have some pie."

The three little kittens put on their mittens
And soon ate up the pie;
"Oh, mother dear, we greatly fear our
    mittens we have soiled."
"What! Soiled your mittens, you naughty
    kittens."
And they began to sigh.
"Meeow, meeow, meeow."
Then they began to sigh.

The three little kittens, they washed their
  mittens
And hung them out to dry.
"Oh, Mother dear, do not you hear our
  mittens we have washed."
"What! Washed your mittens, you good little
  kittens,
But I smell a rat close by."
"Meeow, meeow, meeow,
We smell a rat close by."

This rhyme appeared in Eliza Follen's *New Nursery Songs for
All Good Children* in 1853. It is thought to be traditional.[1]

---

1. Mulherin, Jennifer, editor, Popular Nursery Rhymes, Granada
Publishing, 1984, pp. 150, 151.

Lessons from Mother Goose

MAKING MITTENS
Art

Materials: a variety of printed material cut into rectangles
black marking pens
scissors
stapler
clothesline or rope
optional: needle and yarn

Method: Each child is given a pair of folded material rectangles. With fingers together, the child traces a "mitten" around his hand with a marking pen, onto each folded piece of material. To insure that the material remains folded, it may be pinned or held together with a gem clip before being cut out.

     The teacher then staples the two pieces of each mitten together. These may be hung on a clothesline in the room or tacked on the bulletin board.

Optional: If children wish to wash the mittens, they must be sewn first with a "whipped" stitch.

MATCHING MITTENS
Language Arts

Each child is asked to bring a pair of mittens to school (gloves are acceptable). They are all placed in a box and mixed up. Children take turns matching pairs.

MITTEN MATH
Mathematics

The teacher prepares one mitten card for each player. Each mitten is divided into 16 segments, and a math problem (totalling from 1 to 10) is written in each segment. No two mittens should have their problems in the same order.

16 answer cards, labeled with a number from 1 to 10, are prepared.

The caller picks an answer card and calls out the number. When the player finds a problem on his/her mitten that matches the answer card, he/she covers that space. The first to cover a row horizontally or vertically wins.

Suggestion: Addition, subtraction, multiplication, or division problems may be used according to the developmental level of the children. For very young children, chips may be passed out to assist in addition or subtraction.

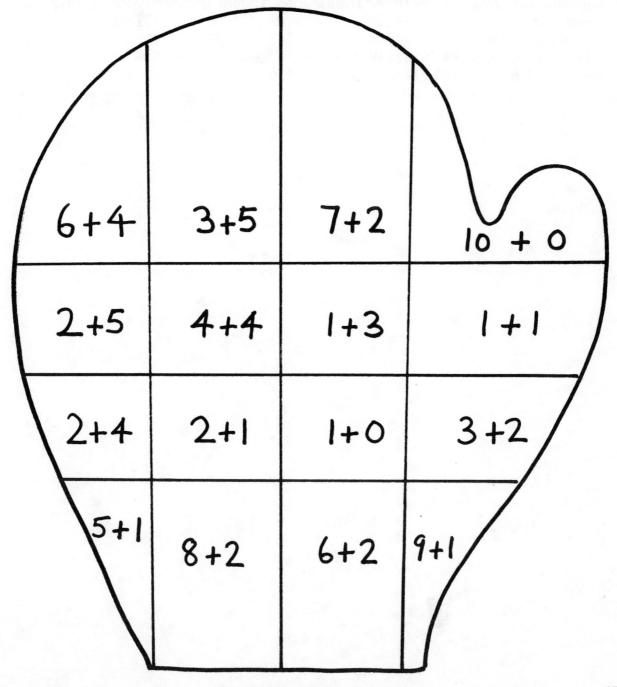

Lessons from Mother Goose

BIBLIOGRAPHY

Baring-Gould, William S. and Ceil, *The Annotated Mother Goose,* Bramhall House, 1962

Commins, Elaine, *Bloomin' Bulletin Boards,* Humanics Ltd., 1984

Commins, Elaine, *Early Childhood Activities,* Humanics Ltd., 1982.

Gregory, O.B., *Henry VIII,* A. Wheaton & Co., Exeter, 1977

Mulherin, Jennifer, editor, *Popular Nursery Rhymes,* Granada Publishing, 1984

Opie, Iona and Peter, *A Family Book of Nursery Rhymes,* Oxford University Press, 1964.

Opie, Iona and Peter, *The Oxford Dictionary of Nursery Rhymes,* Clarendon Press, 1973.

Salzman, L.F., *English Life in the Middle Ages,* Oxford University Press, 1972.

Thomas, Katherine Elwes, *The Real Personages of Mother Goose,* Lothrop, Lee and Shepard, 1930.

Van Loon, Hendrik, *The Songs We Sing,* Simon and Schuster, 1936.

World Book Encyclopedia, Vols. 13 and 14, 1972.